High Desert
of Central Oregon

by

Raymond R. Hatton

High Desert of Central Oregon focuses on the historical geography of these vast windswept lands. This sparsely populated area, lying in the rain shadow of the Cascade spine of Oregon, is a seemingly inhospitable environment. Here, homesteaders, lured by false claims and cheap lands, settled the High Desert of Central Oregon about 1910 and established little-known "communities" such as Imperial, Pringle Flats, Rolyat, Stauffer, Fleetwood, and Fremont.

This is the story of the homesteaders' struggle against adversities of climate and isolation. Skeletal remains of homesteaders' cabins are still part of the desert landscapes. The only small scattered communities that have survived the homestead era are Millican, Brothers, Hampton, Fort Rock and Silver Lake. But the desert land of Central Oregon has a mystique which still lures people—visitors who know intimately its history, its geology, its haunting beauty. Some are especially aware of the relics of the desert's earliest inhabitants, the Indians.

High Desert of Central Oregon takes the reader into the desert to experience the landscape in its changing moods and to explore the sagebrush, juniper and rimrock that characterize much of the area. It traces a prehistoric river across ancient lake beds and recounts the story of the discovery of ancient Indian sandals and other artifacts in Fort Rock Cave, on the former shores of a vast lake. It includes an account of a nineteenth century discovery which brought attention to the desert lands from the scientific world, but is little known to Oregonians today—and examines the story behind a "Lost Forest."

Cover Photograph
Fort Rock with homesteader's cabin in foreground,
courtesy Oregon State Highway Department.

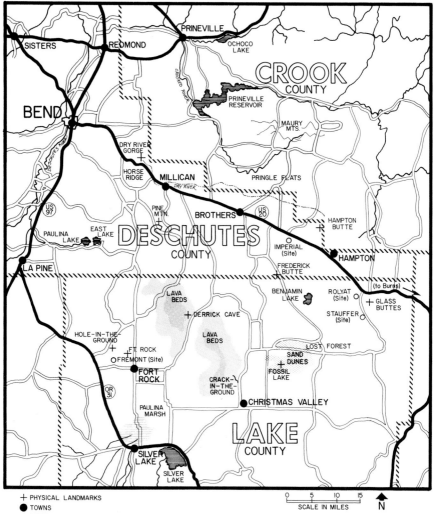

SISTERS
REDMOND
PRINEVILLE
OCHOCO LAKE

CROOK COUNTY

CROOKED RIVER
PRINEVILLE RESERVOIR

BEND
MAURY MTS.

DRY RIVER GORGE
HORSE RIDGE
MILLICAN
DRY RIVER
PRINGLE FLATS

PINE MTN.
BROTHERS
US 20
HAMPTON BUTTE

US 97
PAULINA LAKE
EAST LAKE
DESCHUTES COUNTY
IMPERIAL (Site)
HAMPTON

LA PINE
FREDERICK BUTTE
(to Burns)

LAVA BEDS
BENJAMIN LAKE
ROLYAT (Site)
GLASS BUTTES

DERRICK CAVE
STAUFFER (Site)

HOLE-IN-THE-GROUND
LAVA BEDS
LOST FOREST

FT. ROCK
FREMONT (Site)
SAND DUNES
FOSSIL LAKE

FORT ROCK
CRACK-IN-THE-GROUND
CHRISTMAS VALLEY

OR 31
PAULINA MARSH
LAKE COUNTY

SILVER LAKE
SILVER LAKE

+ PHYSICAL LANDMARKS
● TOWNS
○ SITES

0   5   10   15
SCALE IN MILES
N

HIGH DESERT
of CENTRAL OREGON

Raymond R. Hatton

Binford & Mort

Thomas Binford, Publisher

2536 S.E. Eleventh • Portland, Oregon 97202

High Desert of Central Oregon
Copyright©1977 by Binford & Mort, Publishers

Printed in the United States of America
Library of Congress Catalog Number: 77-85393
ISBN: 0-8323-0298-8 (hardcover); 0-8323-0299-6 (softcover)

First Edition 1977

The following have graciously granted permission to reprint material quoted in this volume: The American Geographical Society, New York, for excerpts from *The Pioneer Fringe* by Isaiah Bowman. Copyright 1931 by The American Geographical Society. Kathy Bowman, Bend, for her unpublished manuscripts, "A Day on the High Desert," "Glenn Cabin," "Brothers" and "Silver lake." Binford and Mort, Publishers, Portland, for an excerpt from *East of the Cascades* by Phil F. Brogan. Copyright© 1964 by Binford & Mort. University of Oregon library for excerpts from "The Historical Geography of the Fort Rock Valley, 1940-41" by James S. Buckles (MA Thesis). Hutchinson Publishing Group Limited, London, for excerpts from *Fragrance of Sage* by Agnes Campbell, published by John Long, Ltd., Publishers, London, 1930. Maurite C. Polhemus for excerpts from *Frontier Doctor* by Urling C. Coe. Copyright 1940 by Macmillan Publishing Co., Inc., New York. The J.K. Gill Co., Portland, for an excerpt from *Oregon Geology* by Thomas Condon. Copyright 1910 by the J.K. Gill Co., Portland. The University of Chicago Press for excerpts from "Fossil Lake, Oregon" by E.D. Cope in the *American Naturalist*, November, 1889. Elizabeth T. Hobson, San Antonio, Texas, for an excerpt from *Honey in the Horn* by H.L. Davis. Copyright 1935 by Harper & Brothers, New York and London. Edwin A. Eskelin, Fort Rock, for excerpts from the unpublished "History of the Eskelin Family," 1974. Metropolitan Press, Portland, for excerpts from *Desert Poems* by Ada Hastings Hedges, 1930. The Caxton Printers, Ltd., Caldwell, Idaho, for excerpts from *The Oregon Desert* by E.R. Jackman and R.A. Long.© 1964 by The Caxton Printers, Ltd. John Wiley & Sons, Inc., New York, for an excerpt from *A Geography of Man* by Preston E. James. Copyright 1949, 1951, © 1959 by Ginn and Company, Boston. All Rights Reserved. Random House, Inc., Alfred A. Knopf, Inc., New York, for excerpts from *Klondike Kate* by Ellis Lucia, published by Ballantine Books, a division of Random House, Inc. © 1962 by Ellis Lucia. Lewis L. McArthur and The Oregon Historical Society for an excerpt from *Oregon Geographic Names* by Lewis L. McArthur, published by The Oregon Historical Society, Portland, 1974. Copyright 1928 and 1944 by Lewis A. McArthur. Copyright 1952 and 1974 by Lewis L. McArthur. The State of Oregon Department of Geology and Mineral Resources for excerpts from "Crack-in-the-Ground" by Norman V. Peterson and Edward A. Groh in *The Ore Bin*, Vol. 26 #9, September, 1964. "Hole-in-the-Ground" by Norman V. Peterson and Edward A. Groh in *The Ore Bin*, Vol. 23, #10, October, 1961, and *Geology and Mineral Resources of Deschutes County, Oregon* by Norman V. Peterson, Edward A. Groh, Edward M. Taylor and Donald E. Stensland, 1976. G.P. Putnam's Sons, New York, for an excerpt from *In the Oregon Country* by George Palmer Putnam, published by The Knickerbocker Press, New York, 1915. Copyright by George Palmer Putnam, 1915. Houghton Mifflin Company, Boston, Mass., for an excerpt from *Where Rolls the Oregon* by Dallas Lore Sharp, published by Houghton Mifflin Company, 1914. The Touchstone Press, Beaverton, Oregon, for excerpts from *Wildflowers 2, Sagebrush Country* by Ronald J. Taylor and Rolf W. Valum. Copyright© 1974 by Ronald J. Taylor and Rolf W. Valum. Association of Oregon Geographers for excerpts from "Stauffer" by Don Van Home, published in the *Oregon Geographer*, Vol. 10, #1, Fall 1976.

iv

To Phil F. Brogan, whose half century of journalism in Bend is reflected in *High Desert of Central Oregon*

CONTENTS

ACKNOWLEDGMENTS

I wish to express my gratitude to the Central Oregon Community College Board for granting sabbatical leave which enabled me to devote considerable uninterrupted time for the research in the summers of 1975 and 1976. The library staff at Central Oregon Community College and the Deschutes County Library have been most helpful and cooperative in facilitating the research. Much of the information for this book has come from local newspapers, especially from the Bend *Bulletin*.

Several individuals have assisted me in the compilation of the manuscript. Their help is greatly appreciated. Edward A. Groh and Dr. Bruce Nolf of Bend gave of their time for consultation on the geology of selected landscapes. Bob Paulson and Tom Oller assisted in the reproduction of many photographs. Peggy Sjogren is thanked for her fine drafting of the maps. Dennis Hill, Bureau of Land Management, Lakeview, provided accounts of Cope's early paleontological discoveries at Fossil Lake. Miss Josephine Godon, Fort Rock, and Mr. K.C. McOmie of Bend allowed me to use various issues of the *Fort Rock Times*. Photographs used in the book, other than my own, came from several different sources; each source is identified.

Christine Bohl, Doris Grady, Karen Kinder, Anita Lanning, Margaret Leone, Sue Lindbo and Bea Youngs all helped at different times with typing the first draft of the manuscript. Special thanks are due Doris Grady and Anita Lanning for their patience and persistence in typing the final copy of the manuscript.

Phil F. Brogan, a long-time Bend resident and author of *East of the Cascades*, not only offered suggestions but kindly read the completed manuscript. The manuscript was also read by Dr. Ward S. Tonsfeldt and Keith R. Clark of Central Oregon Community College. Their helpful suggestions and corrections are appreciated. In addition, the author greatly appreciates the work performed by Thomas Binford, publisher, and Laura Phillips, editor, of Binford & Mort, who helped create the book from the manuscript.

R.H.

INTRODUCTION

This is your desert, with its strange vast moods[1]

Central Oregon, Bend in particular, has now been re-discovered. No longer isolated from other parts of Oregon, no longer far removed from the populous areas of California, it has become more and more a desirable place in which to vacation and to live. Increased leisure time, affluency, improved highways and advertising have contributed to the deluge of tourists descending on the area. Higher crime rates and deterioration of urban environments have sent families looking for more livable communities in many rural parts of the United States—including Oregon.

Increased tourism and population migration to Central Oregon have had and continue to have tremendous impacts on the local environments. The once quiet out-of-the-way campgrounds are no longer known only to local people. Mt. Bachelor, Inc., now boasts six chairlifts and is fast achieving national, even international, reputation for its good powder skiing. Tourism, once largely confined to the summer season, has become a major year-round economic activity in Bend. Major highways throughout Central Oregon, not long ago relatively free of congestion, are frequently clogged with cars, campers, trailers, and pickups hauling motorcycles up front or towing boats in summer or snowmobiles in winter.

Vast stretches of vacant sagebrush and juniper lands have been claimed, staked and carved up for rural subdivisions. Mobile homes and ranch-style dwellings now dot the landscapes from Madras to LaPine, and from Sisters to Prineville. Bend, once a small, peaceful town east of the Cascades, has developed into the "metropolis" of Central Oregon. With its residential, commercial and industrial growth expected to continue at a rapid rate, many local residents fear out-of-state take-over of their pine, juniper and sagebrush country.

In places, it appears that only federally owned lands are holding back the flood of migrants who come to retire, to find employment or to seek a less harried life than that encountered in large urban areas. Throughout this century, irrigation water has become available to large, thirsty acreages in the northern parts of Central Oregon. The resulting changes are much in evidence as green replaces brown, cattle replace the sagebrush, homes are substituted for rocks, and people for rabbits and deer.

Resort living, reflecting, in part, increased affluence and mobility for many Americans, but also reflecting man's attempt to associate more closely, to play, live and build with the natural environment in mind, is now an accepted part of the Central Oregon scene. Meanwhile, wilderness areas, protected from some of the more undesirable attributes of man—his machines, his settlements, his exploitation of resources—are seemingly becoming more accessible to more people every year, to the point that some wilderness areas are in jeopardy of having "no vacancy" signs, and permits are passports to those open spaces.

Mention the name "Central Oregon" to a sampling of Oregonians both east and west of the Cascades, ask what first comes to mind, and you are apt to receive a variety of responses. To winter sports enthusiasts, skiing—alpine or nordic—may be their immediate response. Others may suggest hunting or fishing. Camping may be the first choice of some. Yet other responses could include roaming the vast desert lands, hiking the wilderness areas of Central Oregon, or rockhounding near Madras or Prineville, or resort living at Sunriver, Black Butte Ranch, or the Inn of the Seventh Mountain. The climate of Central Oregon—noted for its clear, dry air, sharply contrasting seasons, and an abundance of sunshine—may be singled out by many.

The readily accessible volcanic lands—characterized by relatively recent lava flows and by a variety of geological features—are major sources of attractions for visitors and residents of the area. The Cascade skyline, a series of distinctive volcanic peaks rising above a fairly uniform plain, separates western Oregon—with its temperate marine climate and lush, dense forests with an abundance of undergrowth—from the more arid, sparsely populated lands which are symbolic with the name "Central

Oregon." People living in the farming communities of rural Central Oregon may well consider that, at least to them, the region represents irrigated pastures, fields of mint and potatoes, and livestock grazing.

The High Desert of Central Oregon has been described as the "graveyard of homesteaders' hopes. When the better lands of Oregon had been taken up, land-hungry settlers swarmed into this, one of the most inhospitable regions of continental United States. High, arid, treeless, and chill, the country baffled the utmost labors of the homesteaders and destroyed their dream of a new wheat empire."[2]

Today, new dimensions have been added to the concept of the High Desert. If you wish to become familiar with this land, you should spend a weekend exploring the vast lands east of Bend. Look for arrowheads, wander through abandoned homesteads, listen to the ever-present wind as it passes over sand and sagebrush. If you go in winter, imagine the bitter chill that confronted homesteaders, many living in tents before their cabins were constructed. In summer, endure the scorching afternoon heat.

Linger to witness the sun lowering over rimrocks, silhouetting against lone junipers and casting long shadows through the ubiquitous sage. Photograph the glorious sunsets. Stay overnight in the desert and witness the myriad stars in the clear desert air—air perfumed by the fragrance of sage. Get up early to watch the sun's rays fill the eastern sky before tinting pink the white-capped Cascade volcanoes far to the west. Notice how the nearby desert landscapes change as the sun's rays are cast on the higher hills and rimrocks before flooding ancient lake beds with light and warmth.

For you who have yet to see Central Oregon, I hope this book will better prepare you for the visit. For you, who live there, or for visitors who have come to know the region intimately, it is my hope that this book will bring added pleasure on future excursions.

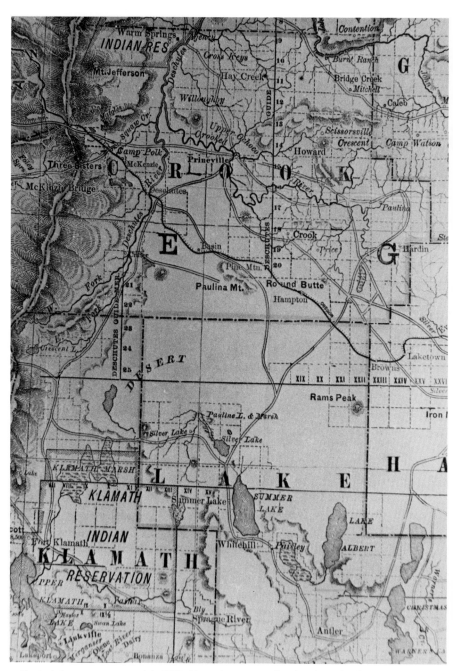

Central Oregon as mapped in 1889. Note the proposed railroad north of Pine Mountain and the cartographer's way of marking the land north of Silver Lake as "Desert." Farther east, a large void fills the desert lands. Bend did not exist as a town in 1889. (University of Oregon map library)

1.

DESERT COUNTRY

The desert lands of Central Oregon, southeast of Bend, are generally less well known and much less frequently visited than other landscape regions of the area. Undoubtedly, to many people the name "desert" denotes a lifeless, uninteresting area shunned by man and largely devoid of both plant and animal life. Many even dispute the notion that Central Oregon has a desert. Botanists, in defining the vegetation of the vast arid lands of Central and Eastern Oregon, consider them as steppes. The early twentieth-century volumes, *An Illustrated History of Central Oregon*, in describing the large territories of Crook County—which included all of Deschutes County until 1916— state:

The so-called "desert lands" cover an area of about 30 townships in the south central part of the county. The term "desert" is not properly applied to these lands. It is not a desert under the ordinary acceptance of the word. The land is generally level, broken here and there by low ridges and occasionally a volcanic butte or crater extinct ages ago, and sloping to the northward with the general watershed of the Deschutes and Crooked rivers which bound the desert on two sides of this triangular form. A large part of it produces a scattering growth of red juniper, valuable for fire wood and fence posts; thousands of acres of black sage and chamise, valuable for nothing except as an indication of the fertility of the soil and above all, that

1

which makes Crook famous for its livestock—bunch grass being in profusion everywhere. Except a few springs near the hills there is absolutely no water to be found in the section. Hence the name "desert."[3]

Actually, very few parts of any desert are entirely barren. The typical desert scene, anywhere in the world, includes a cover of low shrubs and grasses. Furthermore, "the concept of a desert as a vast expanse of shifting sand is incorrect for actually only a relatively small proportion is composed of rocky plateaus channeled by dry water-courses or basins surrounded by barren mountains."[4]

Certainly, cartographers compiling maps on Oregon as early as 1889 recognized the existence of desert lands in Central Oregon. Later maps of the same area show a "Great Sandy Desert" covering considerable territory between Glass Buttes and Christmas Lake Valley. As the name, "Great Sandy Desert," fell into disuse, the plateau region east of the Millican Basin to the south of Hampton and Glass Buttes and Pine Mountain was termed the High Desert.[5] During the homesteading era in Central Oregon, virtually all of the dry lands east of the Deschutes River were termed "desert," including parts of the juniper landscapes just east of Bend.[6]

Dictionaries generally define a desert as dry, barren country unable in itself to support considerable animal or plant life. Some describe it as wild and desolate wasteland. This volume focuses on what to many is a desolate part of Central Oregon; yet, to others, the desert offers them adventure, tranquility, solitude and beauty. The settlement and abandonment of the Millican, Hampton Valley, and Fort Rock areas by early twentieth century homesteaders is examined from a literary and historical perspective. Finally, some of the unique landscape changes and scenes of the Central Oregon desert are described.

Many of the landscape features that are to be seen throughout much of the High Desert are described by Agnes Campbell, an author who had obviously become greatly attached to these lands:

High desert! Wind and sand and sage brush, unquickened by
the hand of industry, empty save for the scurrying rabbits in the
sage! A geological story written in lava flows and rim rocks and
basalt cliffs recently enough that any chance passer-by may
read it if he will. The wind, invisible inhabitant of empty space,
has a way of snatching at the dust and whirling it aloft in
slender columns that travel with incredible speed. Only by the
dust it plays with is this lawless spirit to be seen. Yet it is there,
wild, mocking, shrieking Thing that dances gleefully. It is proud
and jealous, this spirit of the wastes, which to know is to love—
or to hate.

One must be one with it, or find oneself overwhelmed by
vastness. Once touched by desert madness all other lands seem
tame and dull, mountains imprison, the beauty of a cultivated
country becomes vapid and pale. One cannot write of the
desert, prodigal as it is of distance and of space, in a few short
sentences. Words become inadequate to convey to those who
have not felt it, the absolute enthrallment.[7]

Here and there, increased precipitation on the windward
slopes of hills and ridges has enabled the stubborn juniper to
grow in sparsely scattered stands. Otherwise, except for rimrocks and buttes, there is nothing that impedes the vistas across
the gray landscapes except when summer haze or blowing dust
fills the desert air. Where, then, is the beauty of the desert? Let
us examine a "day" on the High Desert and relive the experiences of others—those who have expressed their perceptions.

Kathy Bowman vividly describes a day on the High Desert:

Sunrise sneaks in early on the High Desert. If the night has
been clear, consequently cold, the pale yellow film of light
gradually brightens behind the time-worn buttes at the far
eastern end of the grey-green basin of ancient Lake Millican,
which is now long gone. . . .

Suddenly an intense, blinding, yellow-white forest fire,
strangely smokeless, appears along the crest of a distant ridge.
The butte itself, by contrast, grows darker.

As the shadowed basin finally receives the first stabs of sunlight, quick flecks of minute fire are flashed back to the sun

A small dustdevil skips along a dirt road in the "Rolyat Country" on the High Desert 80 miles east of Bend.

Miles and miles of sagebrush. Remnants of winter's snow provide moisture for otherwise parched soils. Photo taken in "Stauffer Country."

from fine-grained, glittering crystals of hoar frost. The color of the ancient lake bed changes from evening's dark purples to the soft, clean, grey-green of sage, barely dampened by the sparse night condensation. . . .

As the wildfire becomes a shining disk low in the sky, the eastern ridges become lighter in color. As this circle of fire progresses higher into the sky, its commanding power over life in the desert becomes apparent. Heat waves and microparticles of dust begin to rise, hanging low over the silent sage. Dust and a grey-brown hotness, settling over the silent sage, is relieved visually only by the hard, dark clumps of junipers in the distance. What desert life that stirs moves quietly in the hot dustiness, unless the threat of danger necessitates a quick scurry for the unprotective cover of the scratchy branches of sage. Most who travel this way come at this time of the day. . . .

As the heat of the day slackens with the westward decline of the sun, a unique phenomenon takes place—the sun sets in the east as well as in the west.

To the east, a more subtle, yet equally beautiful display of colors, both soft and bright, takes place. The grey-green expanse of sage and settling dust begins to turn a bright, glowing orange-gold sea, bounded by the distant lavender buttes and redefining the ancient lake basin. As the sun sinks behind the peaks to the west, the rays are removed from the Valley floor and focused instead on the distant buttes in the east.

The western sunset is usually of spectacular beauty. If clouds have formed, they are wildly streaked with yellow, orange and pink. The snowcapped western peaks are silhouetted against a blazing sky, while the foothills of the volcanoes turn blue-black.

As the last rays of the sun recede, the hills and valley blend into grey-blues and purples, slowly followed by a clear black night strewn with enormous stars. The huge disc of the soft orange, full moon rises over low ridges. The night creatures stir, their presence represented by the thin, high voices of a coyote serenading the dark, silent sage.[8]

These same high-desert sunrises and sunsets brought joy to the life of Klondike Kate (legendary character of the West who lived in Bend and the High Desert of Central Oregon for many years; she died in 1957 and her last request was to have her ashes scattered among the sagebrush of her former homestead on the High Desert):

> She swept and scrubbed the little shack daily, to keep back the dust and sand. Her hands were blistered and her shoulders ached from grubbing sagebrush and packing rocks and her back and chest pained so that she feared she might have tuberculosis. Several times she was on the verge of quitting but Kate was a stubborn gal and besides, the desert enchanted her.
>
> When her heart was numb with emptiness, it was flaming desert sunsets that gave her a renewed lift. Kate would stand silently watching this sight evening after evening, enraptured by the changing hues of twilight over the land and the wide sky, followed by the jewel-like stars at arm's length and the rising of the huge silver moon which when it was cold, sparkled on the frost like fairy dust scattered across clumps of sage. "I guess if it had not been for the sheer beauty of the desert sunsets, I'd have quit," she later recalled.[9]

In more recent times, a resident of Portland traveling across the dry lands of Central Oregon was so impressed by a desert sunset that he was prompted to describe the scene in a letter to the editor of the Bend *Bulletin*:

> I was not prepared for the flaming spread of color from one end of the sky to the other, for the broad reaches of crimson, saffron and orange engulfing the earth, for the pine trees standing black against a scarlet sky.[10]

The desert night is also not without its mystique. Bend's Dr. Coe, who frequently traveled throughout the desert of Central Oregon to treat ill or injured patients on their homesteads, wrote:

> I stopped the team to consider the situation. Although the urgency of the call was uppermost in my mind, I was caught in the spell of the enchanted desert night, and sat for a moment thrilled and silent, listening to the ponderous stillness of the sleeping desert. There was no sound but the breathing of the horses and the faint rustle of a gentle gust of desert breeze.

Then just ahead and to the right of us a violent burst of weird coyote howls suddenly shattered the tranquil stillness. The swelling, expanding waves of sound rolled across the wide desert, leaping across plain and arroyo to be dashed against the distant rimrock and be hurled back again in reverberating, widening echoes that floated away on the thin desert air and died in the distance in thinning expiring waves.[11]

Central Oregon weather is noted too for its changeability—but also its unpredictability. Out-of-season weather is common. Weather in the high plateau country east of Bend is no exception. In general, winters are cold; summers hot. Blizzards, duststorms, and thunderstorms add variety to the desert climate. However, it is the timing of such weather phenomena that intrigues the desert dweller and bewilders the unwitting visitor:

There are in reality but two seasons in the high desert, one a queer mixture of the other. For January may have days of blazing sunshine, May mornings disclose a skirt of snow, and August nights be sharp with frost. There is no burgeoning of bush and bough in springtime, no colorful departing year. Only one who knows the desert knows when to look for flowers in bloom, sand lilies and chamise; when to expect the tender, soft grey-green of new sprouts on the sage. Those plains which look all of a piece, dead monotonous, dull and grey, have in fact an infinite variety of detail, changes so delicate, design of such intricacy that to one whose eyes are open it possesses vastly more charm, more fascination than the anticipated variation of less subtle lands.[12]

An important part of the desert (and juniper) landscapes is the dusty, grey sagebrush. Actually the word sagebrush refers collectively to several species of low shrubs distributed throughout the semiarid regions of North America: "Among these species, tall sagebrush (*Artemisia tridentata*) has the broadest ecological tolerance and thus can survive under the greatest range of environmental conditions."[13]

The size of the sagebrush varies widely throughout the desert lands of Central Oregon. Near Glass Buttes, south of the Bend-

Healthy-looking sagebrush (*Artemisia tridentata*) in the Fort Rock Country. Sagebrush is one of the major botanical landscape features of the arid lands of Central Oregon.

Sagebrush plains extend to time-worn hills. Juniper fence posts indicate that man has made past attempts to wrestle with the desert. (Bill Van Allen photo)

Burns Highway, there exists an almost impenetrable forest of tall sagebrush half obscuring the decaying frame structure of an abandoned homestead. Elsewhere in poor, rocky soils, the sagebrush grows to barely one or two feet in height. The ecology of the tall sagebrush is summarized by Taylor and Valum:

Tall sagebrush has evolved a number of adaptions "designed" to increase the efficiency of water absorption and retention under semiarid conditions. The leaves are small with a limited surface area from which water can be lost through transpiration. Also, they are densely covered with grayish hairs which further reduce transpiration, both by reflecting sunlight and therefore cooling the plant and by inhibiting the movement of dry wind across the leaf surface. Furthermore, the plants become somewhat dormant during the drier part of the year thus conserving water. "Rapid" growth resumes in the late winter and moist spring.

Tall sagebrush also has an efficient root system, consisting of small, widely dispersed, shallow roots which absorb water rapidly before it can evaporate following rainstorms, and coarse, penetrating roots which draw water from reservoirs deep beneath the earth's surface.

Although tall sagebrush has a broad ecological tolerance, it is not necessarily a stronger competitor. In the more moist extremes of its ecological range it tends to be replaced by grasses and/or other shrubs, or even trees. However, the decay of its fallen leaves results in the release of toxic compounds that apparently limit the growth of some would-be competitors.

Other environmental factors also influence competitive ability. Under conditions of heavy grazing, competing grasses are depressed and sagebrush growth is thereby enhanced. In contrast, fire selectively destroys the dry woody sagebrush plants favoring increased density of grasses.

The minute flowers of sagebrush are produced during late summer or early fall in numerous small yellowish heads. Although insect pollination tends to be the rule in most members of the sunflower family (*Compositae*), sagebrush is wind pollinated. This results in an allergic response and associated discomfort by some people and this response is further aggravated by the slow flower production and consequent extension of the flowering period. The volatile chemicals which are responsible for the strong sage odor may have a mild allergenic effect.

Among the most important identifying characteristics of tall sagebrush are leaf, shape and color. The grayish color attributable to dense hairs has previously been mentioned. The shape is wedgelike and, as the name *tridentata* indicates, three-lobed at the broadened tip. However, there are usually a number of more elongated, non-lobed leaves near the branch tips. . . .[14]

There have been several attempts to put the sagebrush "to work." In 1905, a Baker City, Oregon, chemist in hope of using sagebrush oil as a base for perfume and obtaining paper from the shrub itself, stated that "if the cost of production is reduced, farms will be planting sagebrush in their irrigated fields."[15]

A few years later, the economic value of the sagebrush was reported with optimism in the Bend *Bulletin:*

Sagebrush, heretofore, looked upon as valueless, may prove to be one of the big crops of the west, if the information given to the State Publicity and Industrial Commission of Nevada by Chicago chemists proves to be correct. According to the report of Professor Sylvester Sparling of Chicago, 4,000 pounds of sagebrush produced 220 gallons of distillate, and further yielded 350 pounds of charcoal. The distillate contained tar, wood alcohol, acetic acid and several other products. The figures given indicate that the thousands of acres of sagebrush land in the west can be made to produce millions of dollars in products annually if the distilling process now being perfected by the Chicago chemists is employed.[16]

In April, 1910, a further article reported on the start of an actual attempt to use the sagebrush in Central Oregon:

Victor Schrader, wife, four daughters and four sons arrived last week from Davenport, Washington, and have settled on a 320 acre homestead near Hampton Butte. They came from Davenport in their two white steamers, with 1500 pounds of camping outfit, taking a leisurely pace and occupying three weeks with the trip. The last run, from Shaniko, was made in a day.

Mr. Schrader has been in business a number of years in Washington. Some time ago his attention was drawn to the possibility of making sagebrush (artemisia) the hitherto worthless and troublesome arid land shrub, a valuable resource, and in the course of his investigations he received last week a report of recent results accurately stated.

For a plant that will handle 120 tons of sagebrush every 24 hours the cost is estimated to be $70,000 and it would cost $30,000 to operate the plant for three months. The cost of treating the sagebrush would be $3.25 per ton. Each such ton would yield wood alcohol, acetic acid, tar and charcoal of the market value of $23.81, leaving a profit of $20.56 per ton, $740,160 on the 36,000 tons or 740 percent on the investment, and incidentally a good deal of land will have been cleared for cultivation.[17]

As far as I can ascertain, no widespread economic value of the sagebrush has been found. In Central Oregon, as elsewhere, some artistically minded residents of the area shred the shaggy bark from the sturdy, gnarled stem of the sagebrush and put their imagination to work in sandpapering, preserving, and finishing the twisted stems. Along with other natural native materials of Central Oregon—volcanic rocks, obsidian, gem stones, cinders, juniper branches and mosses—the drab sage can be used in a variety of decorative garden landscaping.

Throughout countless square miles of the High Desert of Central Oregon, various species of grasses are widespread and important parts of the landscape. Furthermore, they contribute to the economy of the area in providing grazing for cattle on public and private lands. In places, it is only clumps of bunch grasses that prevent or inhibit erosion of the light pumice soils. Small animals of the desert seek shelter in the grasses.

The ecology and adaption of desert grasses is summarized here:

Strategies of adaptation exploited by grasses are both numerous and effective. The evolution of elaborate anatomical and structural characteristics has enabled grasses to absorb and conserve water efficiently. In addition, most species can tolerate extensive dehydration without permanent tissue damage. Finally, many species are short-lived annuals which are able to complete their life cycle (from seed to seed) during moist periods, thus escaping drought.

Unquestionably, there is no similarly large group of plants so well adapted to the semiarid conditions of the steppe as are the grasses. Grasses have also evolved an efficient system of wind pollination. The sepals and petals which can only interfere with the transfer of pollen by wind have been lost. At the time of pollen release, the stamens become elongated and extend well beyond confining bracts thus enabling the pollen to be freely dispersed by the wind. At the same time, the sticky, pollen-receptive stigmas, with their numerous branches, become completely exposed and "comb" the air for pollen grains.

In spite of extensive and obvious differences among most species, grasses in general tend to look alike and there is some basis for the statement, "if you've seen one grass you've seen them all" or "a grass is a grass is a grass. . . ." The leaves are primarily basal and tufted, and are long, narrow, and parallel-veined. Stems are round and jointed, and are derived from extensively branched root systems or from creeping rhizomes (underground stems). The flowers consist only of stamens and/or pistils and are associated with various chafflike bracts which often have hairlike or bristlelike appendages (awns). The flower(s) and associated bracts are collectively referred to as a spikelet. Spikelets may be borne directly on the stem, as with wheat, or on flexuous branches, as with oats. The fruit is, of course, a grain.[18]

In the last quarter century, considerable work has been done on attempts to improve the desert range for ranchers in the area. Research at the Squaw Butte-Harney Branch experimental station, by agronomists, animal husbandmen and range conservationists, has been done to control sagebrush by spraying, seeding with crested wheatgrass, and fertilized meadows. In the Fort Rock Valley, as we will see later, irrigation water has helped change the landscape scenes. Modern transportation, electricity and the telephone now link what were or still are remote parts of the Central Oregon desert with the rest of the state.

2.

HOMESTEADING THE DESERT

The struggle of man versus nature in the desert is not a success story. Let us turn back the calendar and look in at the desert-homesteading era in Central Oregon. Up to 1890, homesteading in Oregon was essentially confined to the more attractive, fertile, watered lands west of the Cascades. Overland immigrants bypassed or traveled through the much less attractive desert territory east of the Cascades. However, by the turn of the twentieth century, settlers—encouraged by the passage of two homestead acts—were drawn to the unclaimed open lands in Central Oregon. The revised homestead act of 1909 granted settlers 320 acres of their own land, providing they paid a ten-dollar fee, occupied the land within six months after filing a claim, and "improved" the claim within five years.

There was little reason, at first, to doubt the success of establishing homesteads in Central Oregon. Reports told of tall, healthy sagebrush and liberal coverings of waist-high bunch grass throughout thousands of acres of desert lands. Rumors of a railroad to Bend and extensions across the desert to Lakeview and to Burns frequently headlined the Bend *Bulletin*. The town of Hampton was to become a main railroad center. Irrigation waters, according to promises, were to bless the arid lands.

Yes, dreams, determination, optimism and later, deception, contributed greatly to the stream of settlers who flocked into

13

Central Oregon. The desert scene that greeted the potential homesteader was described by George Palmer Putnam:

> Picture an unbroken plain of sagebrush. Low hills, a mile distant, are fringed with olive-green juniper trees; all the rest is gray, except the ever blue skies which must answer for the eternal hope in the hearts of the homemaker—God smiles there.
>
> Before the railroads came, I went from Bend southeasterly through what was called the "Homestead Country", and in all the hundred and fifty miles traversed we saw three human habitations: the stockman, George Millican; the horse breeder, Johnny Schmeer; and the sheepman, Bill Brown. The rest of it was sagebrush and jack rabbit.[19]

In her poem, "The Desert Wife," Ada Hastings Hedges vividly portrays the bleak scene confronting homesteaders:

The Desert Wife

> They crossed the final mountain in their path,
> A lofty rampart with a weathered peak,
> Like a forbidding god enthroned, whose wrath
> Would halt the timid and deter the weak.
> The two had come by perilous strands of road
> Festooned like cobwebs up the mountain side—
> He drove his own team in the country's mode,
> And she beside him but three days a bride.
> Hills beyond hills she saw, tier after tier,
> With desolated rounded crests as bare as stone,
> And lost in this wild chaos, far or near,
> Were the few acres they would call their own.
> When heart dismayed her lips pressed back a cry—
> His face was forward and his chin was high.[20]

A further description is provided by Coe:

> At that time Oregon was nearing the peak of its greatest homestead era, with a constant stream of settlers pouring in

from all parts of the country. The agriculture experts of the General Land Office in Washington had made a survey of the high desert country and had classified the land as being suitable for dry farming by the approved methods.

Thousands of antelope, mule deer, coyotes, badgers, bobcats, jack rabbits, sage hens, and other animals and birds roamed its wide expanse free and unmolested. Here the stockmen had thousands of wild horses, cattle and sheep running on the open range throughout the year. About a million and a half acres of this land were segregated by the General Land Office and thrown open to entry under homestead law.

The stockmen at once raised a vigorous protest because their range was being taken away, and assured the Land Office that, although the country was excellent stock range, it was entirely unfit for agriculture. The oldest settlers had found it impossible to raise any kind of stock feed there because there was not sufficient moisture. The agriculture experts thought they knew more about it than the stockmen and paid no heed to their warnings and protest.

The real estate men and locators ran out the section lines and were ready and eager to locate settlers on the three-hundred-and-twenty-acre homesteads for a fee of from one to three hundred dollars, and advertised the free land Uncle Sam was giving away far and wide. What if the old settlers did say the country was too arid for agriculture? The experts in Washington knew better. The locators told prospective settlers that any man with from three to five thousand dollars capital who was not afraid of hardship and hard work could make the land support a family by the time the capital was expended.

New settlers flocked in and were captivated by the new country with its abundant wild life, dry rare air and wonderful climate.[21]

Within a period of two years, homesteaders' residences and farm buildings took shape from Bear Creek Butte on south past Christmas Lake Valley. The Bend *Bulletin* later reported:

The vanguard of the home seekers was generally the heads of families, who, with locators as their guides, moved into the

Several freight liners meet on the desert, and drivers seem to be exchanging gossip. Desolation of the meeting place probably indicates that the meeting was unplanned. (Deschutes County Library photo)

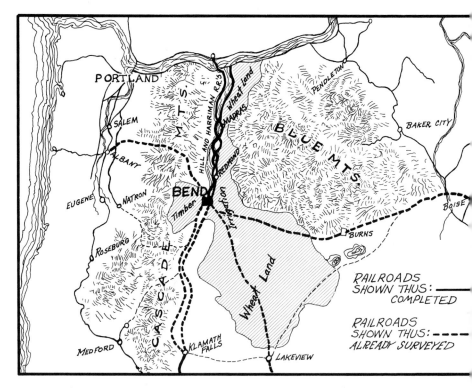

Reproduction of a map included in the Bend *Bulletin*, July 3, 1912, showing the location of Bend in relation to Central Oregon resources. Note that much of the High Desert was then designated to be future "Wheat Lands" with railroads surveyed from Bend to Lakeview and Bend to Boise. Location of Burns has been added to the original map.

16

plateau to make a choice of lands. Then from points as distant as Boston, Mass., moved families and household equipment.

In one week, early in November, 1911, 51 carloads of household goods arrived in Bend by train from distant places. Most of the homeseekers were still without stock and they hired freighters to move their goods to their new homes, generally cabin-like structures.

The town of Hampton experienced a "boom." In 1910, there were only two houses in the town. Two years later, 24 buildings, most of them residences, were counted.

Fences appeared on the high plateau. Sagebrush was removed, and crops were planted. New arrivals had been cautioned by old timers that for a safe crop for their animals they should plant rye. The new arrivals were also told to plant maize. Even field peas were recommended. Rye planted in September, 1911, was up before the first snow of November came.

New arrivals faced rather stark conditions that fall. It was a dry fall following a damp September. The settlers soon found the need of water. It was presumed that water would be found a short distance under the surface, but in most areas it was not located until deep wells had been drilled, some 300 feet. From Tulsa, Okla., came the Murphy Bros., professional well drillers, and they said they liked the area.

The rush to the high plateau was due to several factors—principally, the attention directed to Central Oregon by the arrival of the railroads, and predictions that the area would develop into a second prairie wheat bowl. There was also a period of heavy precipitation, and lush vegetation.

Then came difficult times for the hundreds who planned to carve their homes from the high desert wilderness. As early as 1911, one homesteader, for instance, found it difficult to raise potatoes in the highlands. Three times that spring he planted potatoes. Twice they froze. His third crop matured, but the potatoes were only the size of eggs.

Agriculturists, state college men, railway agents and others joined in an effort to recommend crops that might flourish in the high desert, but a period of aridity offset all these efforts.[22]

What were the thoughts and feelings of these homesteaders about the desert? In the author's research on written material relating to the homesteading of the Central Oregon desert, it is significant to note that despite mention of desert beauty, most descriptions focused on the reality of the situation. For example, Klondike Kate's experience in "homesteading" the High Desert is described by Ellis Lucia:

But now there was another longing and that was to get back to central Oregon. Even her mother realized that Kate had found peace of mind in that open country east of the Cascades. One day in 1914, a man entered Mrs. Bettis's real estate office and offered to swap a homestead near Bend for something on Puget Sound. It sounded too good to be true, and a deal was quickly made, with Kate tossing some gold coin for encouragement into the bargain. All thoughts of continuing her theatrical engagements were cast aside. Kate was so eager to return to central Oregon that she dropped everything, packed quickly, and said only a hasty goodbye to a few close friends.

She was horrified when first she laid eyes on what she'd acquired sight unseen, in the middle of nowhere on the High Desert, forty miles east of Bend and three miles northeast of a place called Brothers, consisting of a tiny store and a few other shacks. It stood amid oceans of sagebrush, a one-room shack about fourteen by twenty feet. A good hike away stood a flimsy shed, supposed to be the "barn." The empty land of sand, rocks, rats, jack rabbits and rattlesnakes stretched in great rolls in every direction with a ridge of ordinary mountains rising to the east as the only break in the monotony. Kate had acquired a pig in a poke, but if she wanted to get away from people, as she professed, she'd done a first-rate job of it: the High Desert seemed abandoned to sun and wind and rattlesnakes.[23]

While most of the homesteaders arrived in Central Oregon through Shaniko or Bend (or both towns), the following extracts describe landscape scenes, experiences while on overland travel from the John Day country south to Glass Buttes, then westward toward the Deschutes River. It is not difficult to feel part of the journey across the High Desert, perhaps half a century ago:

Homestead on the Central Oregon desert. Weather-worn boards, sagging roof, scattered debris on sagebrush plain are typical landscape scenes.

A desert variety of phlox sharply contrasts dull, gray sagebrush with bleached juniper posts.

Always and always the road, sometimes hardly more than a trail, sometimes made wider by the addition of another vaguely wandering track that joined it, wound on and on through sage and juniper and occasional growths of jack pine, coming from nowhere at all, going on until it dipped out of sight between the edge of the sky and the edge of the earth.

One woke in the mornings in the glory of sunrise, cold and sage-sweet and clear, only to find the road there ready to take up the day's journey. At evening, the riot of color changing as swiftly as the moments drew one from the marks of wheel tracks.

Sheer physical joy could be found in walking away from the weary trail. There they might stand upright upon the dusty earth with never a sign that anyone had passed this way before, and feel themselves first witness to all this unlooked-upon beauty round about. Jim voiced his feeling in the words,

"Just to be alive these days!"
"And to be free," added Marcia.

But she knew that she was not free, never free as long as she must go on and on and ever held captive by that road. In the long hours that stretched between morning and evening, the sky like an inverted blue bowl rested its edges on the endless horizon, and the wind, a fiendish thing that shrieked and moaned and whistled and laughed, scoured the inside of this bowl until it shone with the green-blue patina of burnished bronze. Then the rickety hack top which the wind laid hold of and shook, gave all too inadequate protection against the rays of the sun.

Jim kept a close watch for every sign of animal life. He called Marcia's attention to antelope fleeing into distance like the shadows of animals, coyotes slinking in the sage, or yapping at night from over behind a stretch of rim rock, and little, weazened desert rats that went running down the road in mad panic, only to stop in the wheel tracks and sit watching, making no move to get out of the way after all their terror.

There were rabbits in plenty. One evening early in their journey, Jim had taken his gun and walked away into the sage. Marcia, looking after him, saw him raise it, heard the sharp crack of the report, and waited curiously until he came back

Rimrocks are common physical features of the High Desert, adding scenic qualities
to the vast plains.

Few homesteads on the High Desert have an oasis-like setting as shown above. A few
small streams in the Silver Lake country permit the luxury of trees. (Kathy Bowman photo)

21

dangling the limp, brown form by its ears. That night they had rabbit stew, not at all a bad idea in the way of fresh meat.

Every detail of desert life held interest for Jim, while to Marcia these animals hardly counted as living creatures. In all that wide emptiness only the road and the wind seemed to possess personality—the road resolutely going somewhere, the wind forever mocking it.

Their camp sites varied only in detail, with the ever present desert all around about, the changeless sky above. They stopped beside a spring if it were possible, or near one of those mysterious ice caves. There, descending fifty feet or more through the fallen roof of a lava tunnel that wound beneath the surface of this strange desert, Jim cut from within the black mouth of the cave, blocks of ice to melt by the camp fire. Occasionally after travelling on and on into the dusk in search of water, they were forced to make a dry camp with only guarded supply in the water barrel.

But the mystery of the night when one can look afar to strange worlds, the night when there is no horizon, when the uncertain darkness hides the dust in which one stands, cannot last forever. With dawn one must be up and off again, forever seeking water. Following the cold clear freshness of morning come inevitable empty hours—the road and the wind.

The ranches they passed, dull, grey, hopeless, offered reason enough for pushing on and on and on. At rare intervals the road, topping a bit of rim rock, where the basalt having faulted one edge slips up to form a ridge, brought them into sight of a group of houses and corrals far away across the plain. The buildings showed distinctly in the clear light, but never seemed to grow bigger as the wagon crept toward them. Always with a sense of keen anticipation they approached, sometimes to find no more than empty shacks of weathered clapboard, a dry well, a useless windmill clattering brokenly above it—a sad sound in the wind—abandoned corrals, mute evidence that some disheartened homesteader had grown weary of the hopeless struggle with the forces of the desert.

Reading the silent story of desertion, Marcia shuddered and turned away without comment, eager to hurry on. Jim, watching her, knowing the world of plenty from which she came, realized in some degree that stark fear must dwell within her soul, and marvelled at her courage. Or else they approached a ranch unaware that a woman watched her coming from afar, until she welcomed them with eager hospitality to her four bare walls and the meager resources of a frost-bitten garden.

After passing these farthermost outposts of poverty and abandoned hopes, their arrival at the Giddon road house was a never-to-be-forgotten experience. And the woman they met there, Ma Giddon, came to be not only their neighbor, but Marcia's best friend in the years that followed.

The ranch lay at the crossroads beyond Glass Buttes where the highway from east to west met the road that they travelled southward. From a distance they beheld a sight their eyes had not fallen upon for many and many a day—a white house with a red roof—and when they drew nearer, the carefully fenced plot of green grass around it, flowers against the wall, clean curtains at the windows. It just couldn't be, it just couldn't be. Here also one looked at a mirage, which like other mirages seen from a distance, beautiful lakes with trees along the shore, emerald isles in an expanse of blue water, would fade out and disappear at any instant. But it did not vanish, and at length they drew up before the gate.

After supper—a meal eaten at a table with real dishes and with food properly cooked, tasting as food has never tasted before to these two wanderers who have known only camp fare for many days—and after the dishes had been "cleared up," Ma Giddon took Marcia out to the yard that they might visit a little after the fashion of desert women. There she pointed out with much pride the poplar tree. Marcia, newly come from land where green maples grew, and flowering acacias, elm and oaks and a hundred other deciduous varieties, looked upon the pathos of this slim tree with something like tears in her throat. For although it was midsummer, the leaves were yellow as gold and rattled metallic when the wind, forever intruding, came and fingered them.

"It is such a beautiful tree," remarked Ma Giddon, looking at it lovingly as though it were a thing alive. "Poplars are all we can get to grow here, you know. I've been watering this one five years now, ever since I came here to live, and I've hoped some day it will have green leaves on it. But the sun gets too hot, and the soil isn't right, not rich enough, I don't rightly know the reason, but the leaves always turn yellow. It's this country," she went on as Marcia found no word to answer her. "It is home to me now, and there are right friendly folks living in it. But sometimes I do get homesick to see trees with green leaves."

"Trees with green leaves!" How often in the years that followed Marcia herself, who never again saw any such, came to long for the cool graciousness of trees with green leaves.

The direction of the road took them slightly south of west. All day long they travelled down a dry river bed, the sides of which cut off the view. The road, thought Marcia, mocked them again, keeping them in this deep trough, shutting out the country ahead. Late in the afternoon the horses, ever weary, pulled struggling up a sharp turn around the rim rock, and stopped. From that point Jim and Marcia saw an open plain with apparently nothing to interrupt the sweep of country between them and the high Cascades.

There against the sunset, in all the grandeur of glacier and snowfield, the mountains rose, too dazzling in the light to be looked at for long. Toward them Jim O'Vally gazed as one who has suddenly caught the flick of inspiration. After a few moments he turned the team slowly to journey from the top of the rim rock down across the plain.

"Somewhere here?" Marcia, who had watched him, questioned hesitantly. "Somewhere not very far away now. There must be water from the snow on those mountains." [24]

By now the reader should have a self-perception of the desert landscape described above. It is significant to note how the few cultural landscapes stand out against the natural grey desert landscapes. In my desert journeys, small settlements like Brothers, Millican, Hampton, Fort Rock, and Christmas Valley seem magnified close up, but insignificant when viewed from a distance. Irrigated fields, deciduous trees, seem almost artificially placed. Out in the desert itself, away from any settlement, it seemed strange to come across others. Indeed, on several occasions, in the land between US 20 and the Fort Rock Valley, many miles were passed without meeting or seeing anyone. No wonder Marcia, in Campbell's book, had a memorable experience coming across a painted house, "landscaped" with green grass, flowers and a solitary poplar tree.

The optimism and determination of many of the homesteaders was remarkable. The *Bulletin* reported several accounts of such determination when homesteading on the desert was in its infancy. In one article, mention is made of a Bulgarian-born homesteader who was taken twelve miles beyond Millican with a load of lumber, some provisions and a blanket. The temperature was two below zero (Fahrenheit), and the wind was blowing a gale, but the homesteader would not return to Bend. Instead, he made himself "more or less at home in the middle of the sagebrush, with the nearest cabin several miles distant.[25]

Age, apparently, was no object in the homesteading process. Another *Bulletin* article reported the following incident:

William A. Offield, seventy-five years young, drove to Bend from Hood River some weeks ago, looked the country over, liked it, and forthwith took up a 300-acre homestead in the sagebrush country to the southeast.

The old pioneer is as full of enthusiasm as he was "way back in the fifties," when he first came to Oregon. Then, he says, he saw Portland when it was smaller than Bend is now, and had the opportunity to buy acreage in the heart of the present city at prices which now could not purchase country property ten miles distant. Also he had a hand in the founding of Roseburg and Walla Walla, and declares that now he had come to Central Oregon to be in at the making of the big cities of the interior, greatest of all of which he predicts as Bend.

The septuagenarian homeseeker has located on land 79 miles from Bend. There he is living with a small tent as his only shelter, and a sagebrush shack as a sort of storehouse. However, he declares that before many years have passed, his will be suburban property, and neighboring ranches and towns will crowd thick about him. One of the instances of his first advent to the new land was that when he got out there he discovered that he required a pickaxe with which to make a well, and to get one returned the 79 miles to Bend. It is his intention to stay with his land and grow up with the country.[26]

The task of building a home out in the Central Oregon desert was not always easy—mainly due to a lack of nearby available building materials:

> To build this home for their future—for all their future, as a matter of fact—Jim used the materials he found on hand; rough stone for the lower part of the wall, logs cut from the tallest and straightest juniper trees. The wood splintered badly, but by dint of careful selection he gathered together enough that would do. Marcia helped him, working with all the strength she possessed, hacking at the sage roots, bringing smaller stones with her bare hands, piling them up one on the other until there should be a place to use them. For the fireplace she searched out the lava boulders, light and porous. One day they drove almost as far as Glass Buttes for a load of black obsidian, sharp shiny bits picked up at random to use as decoration with some idea of making this house their creation—attractive, something more than a mere shelter.[27]

Travels through the desert today can lead to the remnants of these homestead cabins. At best, they are forlorn and dilapidated. More often than not, wind and vandals have ravaged them, leaving bleached timbers scattered over the pumice soil as the only clues to a former cabin.

The author has spent many hours in the desert looking for, and at, such cabins, and has repeatedly left, wondering what they were like when occupied. The following two descriptions from different sources help portray homestead life in the Central Oregon desert some sixty years ago. The precious value of the few belongings brought with the homesteaders and the attempts to create a homey cabin are described by Agnes Campbell:

> No matter where she might be in the long years she spent away from the high desert, no matter in what house she might be living, what castle or cathedral she might be looking at, Julia Day had only to shut her eyes in order to see, as a picture etched with the biting acid of memory, this cabin home of her early years.

Metal windmill, still intact, groans and creaks in the desert wind. Note the dense sage and (background) juniper-covered hills.

Abandoned cabin—silent testimony to man's lost battle to wrest a living in the High Desert.

27

Once finished, it presented a pleasant, rather rustic appearance, with two windows and a door in front, the almost flat roof projecting beyond the eaves. It seemed as much a part of the landscape as the break in the rim rock, or Black Butte across the canyon. For even the desert will smooth edges, and the ground round about, which mattock and spade left hacked and raw, weathered again to the dull brown of rocks and sand. . . .

Around the cabin Jim built a fence with pickets cut from the splintery juniper nailed close together, which, as he humorously declared, would "turn" Julia Day when she came to the toddling stage, and keep her from wandering off and getting lost in the sage brush.

Inside, the cabin followed a plan simple enough—two rooms, one large, one small, and behind them, through a door opposite the front door, a lean-to kitchen. The great stone fireplace, constructed of Marcia's carefully selected lava rocks outlined with rows of sharp-edged black obsidian, almost filled one end of the larger of the two rooms—the living room.

On that wide mantel-shelf stood the precious treasure books finally unpacked from the long journey in the battered apple box. The list of titles was limited and ordinary enough. It included the poets—Byron, Shelley, Burns—a few biographies, some fiction, and a half-dozen medical books. . . .

The room had simple, home-made furniture—chairs, a bench, a table, which Jim fashioned from the ever-abundant juniper. Marcia performed miracles with flour sacks, washing and bleaching them and then making curtains, a table cover, even a long runner with edges crocheted from the twine of the sacking. . . .

In that room with all its homely makeshifts centered Julia Day's earliest recollections, most vivid among them that of her father sitting before a fire of juniper boughs that burned with a crackling blue flame in the cavern of the fireplace while the winter wind howled and whistled outside—sitting there resting from the day's work, nursing the bowl of an old black pipe in one hand while with the other he turned already long familiar pages.

He seemed to her youthful eyes a man of many years just as her mother seemed very much a grown-up lady.

Yet in the days to come, when she stood once again in the well-loved rooms after long absences and recalled the early beginnings of life, she knew that they could not have been old at all, must indeed have been young to have had the courage to face life alone in the high desert. [28]

H.L. Davis was not too impressed with the appearance and comfort of the homesteader's cabin:

It was true that most of their improvements did nothing to enhance the beauty of the landscape, which was nothing extra to start with. What was the original reason for the invention of the homestead style of architecture it would be hard to say. It couldn't have been comfort, for the half-inch board walls leaked heat in winter and were furnaces in summer. It certainly wasn't looks, for they were the ugliest objects in sight, so much uglier even than the naked plowed ground that stood out on it like pimples. It wasn't availability of material, for the country around had tons of stone and adobe, either of which could have been organized into a fairly sightly scattering of residences.

The homestead houses were built of undressed lumber, which had to be shipped first by railroad from the timber belt and then hauled south a hundred and thirty miles across the mountains by wagon, the trip taking, as a general thing, from eight to ten days. Bad roads accounted for the slow time, and they were unavoidable. If they had been good, the land wouldn't have been found open for entry.

Old Carstairs and his wife, with whom Clay stayed while he looked around the land that was left open, had been there longer than anybody else, but their house was no better. It was rough cull-lumber with the cracks slatted up, rooms a religious eight feet square with one small window apiece, and the floor set up four feet off the ground because it had been too much trouble to scrape it level and build down on it. It also furnished a place to store articles of value such as old harness, broken mowing-machine parts, barrels that had come apart, unused length of rope and wire, an assorted collection of rusty nails and staples and old gunny sacks, and a couple of washtubs that were going to be mended as good as new when anybody could remember to buy solder in town.

The ceilings were built low for warmth, though it would have been twice as effective to bank earth up under the floor so drafts couldn't blow through the knotholes. The water-supply was a spring with the wash-house built around it. Old Carstairs had put down an artesian well and it spouted profusely, but he used its water only for stock, and mostly it ran wild on the ground and made several acres of mud which were of no use for anything. . . .

The Carstairs' furniture was on a little more elaborate scale than the house. There were several rocking-chairs carved with flurrididdles and adorned with quantities of brass tacks and headrests made out of varicolored ribbon; a center table of which the legs represented birds; claws, each grasping a yellow glass cue-ball; and a porcelain lamp with a globe painted with a marine landscape so the light would shine through it. There was a stereopticon rig with views of an apple-orchard in bloom in Michigan, Niagara Falls in winter, Santiago Bay at sunset, hauling artillery on the walls of Peking and the Meeting of the Waters of Killarney. There were two books, one called *Royal Path of Life*, and the other the *San Francisco Horror of Earthquake, Fire and Famine*, and there was a faint but piercing smell of stale food about the whole place because the kitchen was so arranged that drafts carried through it to the rest of the house. The diet was corn-meal mush, pancakes and fat bacon for breakfast, baking powder biscuits, fat bacon, potatoes, and beans the rest of the time except when the neighbors got together and went whackers on killing a beef. [29]

The plight and desperation of the homesteaders soon became apparent—sometimes more quickly to outsiders than to the settlers themselves. Following a journey from Bend to Burns in 1913, a Professor D.C. Sharp wrote in a magazine article, which was reported on in the *Bulletin* at a later date:

I have seen many sorts of desperation but none like that of men who attempted to make a home out of three hundred and twenty acres of High Desert sage . . . but going out into the desert with a government claim and the necessary plow, the necessary wire fence, the necessary years of residence, and other things made necessary by law, to say nothing of those required by nature and perhaps by marriage, is to pay all too dearly for death and to make one's funeral a needlessly desolate thing. A man plowing the sage! His woman keeping the shack—a patch of dust against the dust, a shadow within the shadow, and nothing then but sage and sand and space.[30]

The homestead era in the Central Oregon desert lasted only a few years, and like the desert flowers, it quickly sprouted, bloomed, then faded. What happened? Why did homesteading, for the most part, fail? Several factors, many interrelated, account for its failure. At first glance, it seemed that relatively little was expected from the homesteaders in order to secure title to the land. In addition to the filing fee, the land had to be lived on for five years, and it had to be improved—perhaps with a cabin, barn, corral, and fences. In five years a final title to the land was made after filing papers and paying a fee that ranged from $26 to $34.

By 1900, most of the best lands in the U.S. were taken. Central and Eastern Oregon desert lands were included in the "leftovers." Little scientific knowledge of the land was available. Furthermore, prior to settlement, the land was deceptively attractive:

From the Paulina Mountains and the Fremont Forest reserve, stretching East beyond the horizon, is a scope of bunch grass plains, considered by the stockmen to be the best range now left in the state. The land is nearly free from rock, and junipers are scattered at wide intervals. It only needs the plow to be transformed into a valley dotted with farms, if possible a more beautiful country than at present. In many places water has been found at a depth of only a few feet.[31]

Climatological records of the area were generally lacking. That the climate was arid was generally known, but the early settlers came at a time of above-normal precipitation. (The average precipitation for Bend, 1902-1912, was 14.77 inches, nearly three inches above the long-term average.) Even after the peak of settlement, 1912-1917, precipitation was above normal in four out of six years and only slightly below normal in the other two years.

From her long personal experience, Ada Hastings Hedges describes the variable weather on the desert:

> A desert's subtlety was known that year
> In gossamer rains of silver tissue spun,
> That scarcely touched the earth to disappear
> As vapour curling upward in the sun;
> Marked in the cool mirage with lakes of blue,
> A taunting dream that perished on the air,
> And in the snow's brief beauty that withdrew
> To leave the hills again to grey despair.
> One snow was deep, and rabbits reaching higher,
> More starved than usual, the natives said,
> Girdled the bark above the bands of wire,
> And in the spring they found their trees were dead.
> The wind blew dust to make her cleaning vain,
> But never any downpour for the grain. [32]

Isaiah Bowman, who in 1930 conducted research into the pioneer settlement of vast areas of the Western United States, wrote:

If the land were productive under tillage it would have been demonstrated then. But the crops for even this favorable five-year period were below the normal for successful dry farming. Abandonment of the area was already in train when the World War came and drew off the young men who composed the greater part of the new population. That proved to be the finishing touch, and the High Desert reverted to sage except where the large size of the holdings and the better location of some of the cultivated tracts permitted a farming-ranching type of occupation to succeed.

Stepping across the outer limit of possibilities to experiment with land is characteristic of every region where the marvels of dry farming and the recurrence of wet years bring temporary and local success. The story gets about that money is easy to make on cheap land. Superficially a poor farm may look much like a good one. Experimentation with crops and tillage methods is the key to occupation of any sort. It runs right through the history of the semiarid West. And it is small wonder that there seems to be no limit to land occupation when so much has already been done that once appeared to be impossible.

The settlers were justified in believing the land good for the dry farming, seeing what a dry-farming technique had done in sagebrush country in Washington and Montana. They could not be expected to know that the summers were drier than in other treeless regions that produced grain. Snowcapped peaks were on the Western horizon. The main streams ran full. On the slopes of the Cascades and spreading out over the higher border of the adjacent plains were magnificent stands of Western yellow pine. Explorers had reported the surfaces of basins and uplands covered with a bunch grass as thick as a meadow.

Settlers poured into central Oregon long before there was a railroad. The first comers of the seventies were stockmen. The desert east of the wooded eastern flanks and fringe of higher piedmont that borders the Cascades was long a sheep and cattle pasture. Bands of sheep and herds of cattle were driven eastward of the mountains to winter in the comparatively warmer grass-covered basins of the desert. In summer, as the lower pastures became hot and dry, they were returned to the higher valleys. A range war was in full swing at the turn of the century in the country east of Prineville and was marked by the slaughter of sheep by cattlemen and the lynching of several sheepmen. Down to 1885 there was still little permanent settlement in the Bend country outside of the scattered ranching communities.[33]

The early 1900's were marked with hope and anticipation. Winter and spring rains brought promise of average crops and optimism throughout the high-desert communities. The promise of a railroad to Bend headlined the *Bulletin* week after week. The eagerly anticipated railroad would, it was believed, increase land values and lower freight costs for grain transport.

By 1905, settlers were moving into the desert east of Bend. Bowman continued:

They were self-styled pioneers invading wilderness and making promising homes. The juniper was cleared off and made into firewood and fence posts, the stumps uprooted and burned, the land cleared of stones, leveled, and plowed. Desert, juniper, sagebrush, experimentation—yet the stream continued. The first regular railway train came into Bend on the night of October 31, 1911. Three years after that, in 1914, ensued the greatest settlement activity in the history of Central Oregon. Thirteen carloads of "immigrants' movables" arrived in the month of March alone. They represented fifteen families from Oregon, Washington, and Idaho. In the same year 15,000 sheep arrived in 65 cars from Coleman, 60 miles to the north. They were on their way to the summer grazing ranges in the mountains and came from their winter quarters in the lower country to the east and north. The transport of sheep by rail between summer and winter feeding grounds is now a practice of considerable extent in the Great Basin country.

Southeastern Oregon proclaimed itself "the greatest free-land opening for the homesteader left in the West"; and by 1910 it was available in 320-acre units—rolling land with a cover of sage and bunch grass. Settlers were enthusiastic about life in a 10 by 12 cabin, wheat outside the door, and domestic water 14 to 20 feet down in the lower sites near the streams. Late in 1910 and early in 1911, in a period of three months, thirty homesteaders' cabins were built within a radius of ten miles of Bend, most of them towards the southeast. "From every prominent hill one can see the clearing work being carried on." Settlers came by motor car, horse team, hack, stage, on horseback, and afoot from the nearest railway station 100 miles away. It wasn't the Klondike "rush" it was pictured to be—that is the booster's note; but it was a movement by scores and by hundreds. It didn't double the wheat output of Oregon, but it did widely extend the limits of unprofitable wheat production.

Most of the entrymen were unmarried. Many of them came from Seattle—city men and women who saw here a chance to make a beginning. By the first of May, 1911, 300 land filings on 96,000 acres were reported in Crook County, which then included Deschutes; and the wave had spread from the lower country right over the High Desert. By the spring of 1912 a note of caution had crept in. Farmers were warned not to depend on one crop or to attempt to cultivate too much. Though the railway had come to Bend, heavy teaming was necessary to get merchandise out into the country and the grain crops back to the railway. It cost 25 cents a mile to haul a ton of farm produce over an ordinary unimproved road. There was much talk of the rates by this route and that, so much a pound or a ton. In July, 1912, it was asserted that the motor truck run to Burns from Bend was "the longest in the country." The crops were good that year, and men clung to the fact that settlers had been in the country southeast of Bend for 40 years.

This was a second wave of pioneering; the first wave came forty years earlier. The first settlers of southeastern Oregon were young men who had come from the east and south in two- and- four-horse wagons, women and children, two and three weeks on the road. The settlers of the Bend region were a backwash from the Willamette Valley region. Having established themselves upon the better agricultural land west of the Cascades, they came back over the mountains to take advantage of the fine pasture for sheep and cattle. Everything had to be freighted for long distances over poor roads. Freighting for the first isolated and distant communities of southeastern Oregon was a picturesque business—wool, hides, grain to Portland by freight wagon, in summer right over the mountains, in winter down the Columbia gorge.

It was hard on the women when the men were off freighting to distant points or out on the range for several weeks at a time. "Our women didn't mind," said my informant; "because that was the kind of life everyone lived," echoed his wife. "We had such remedies as pioneers always have"—which meant that they had next to nothing. The climate is healthful. Epidemics were unknown because of isolated living. They thought of themselves not in a heroic way but as simple folks "looking for a place to make a home, get along, and grow up with the country."[34]

No sooner had the land been settled than problems developed. Urling Coe, a resident doctor of Bend during the time of homesteading the desert, describes the landscape:

Soon squares of dirty brown appeared here and there on the surface of the vast sea of pale green where the settler had cleared his field for sowing of grain. The grain soon sprouted in the rich lava soil, but as soon as its tender new blades thrust their points above the dry clods, the long-eared jack rabbits swarmed over the fields in thousands and waxed fat on the tasty new fare. In some sections the rabbits ate the grain as fast as it appeared above the ground.

The wily coyote and prowling bobcat found the tame chickens of the settler much easier to prey upon than the wild sage hen that whirred away at their sly approach. By the time the settler had purchased a team, wagon and harness, lumber for his shack, wire for his fences to keep the roaming wild stock out of his fields, and supplies for his family, he had made a big hole in his capital, for prices were high so far from the railroad. Then he had to buy feed for his horses and haul his supplies fifty or a hundred miles to get to his land. Water was scarce and was usually hauled several miles by the average homesteader; and if he wanted better firewood than the poor sagebrush, he was obliged to cut the scrubby juniper that grew in scattered patches along the rim rock and high ridges. Juniper made a hot blaze and was excellent material for fence posts since it did not rot like other woods, but it was against the law to cut wood of any kind on the public domain. It was the idea of the land office that the first crop of settlers, who had the most difficult task in opening up the new country, should not be allowed to use the only available material for firewood and fence posts. It should be conserved for future generations and their children and their children's grandchildren—who would have railroads to haul coal to them.

In a few sections where there were not enough rabbits to keep the grain chopped to the ground, it grew rapidly in the fertile lava soil during the spring when there was still a little moisture in the ground. When the hot dry weather came with the approach of summer, it turned yellow and withered before it could head out.

New post offices were established in the homestead country and new towns rapidly sprang up, some with as many as two hundred people. No new doctors came to that part of the country, however. The nearest doctor to me on that side was a hundred and fifty miles away.

The simple life, hard out-of-door work, and wonderful climate made strong men and healthy women, and there was little or no sickness at first. The people were too exhilarated with the fascinating new country and too eager and optimistic for the future to get sick. But with crop failures, lack of proper diet, loss of hope and optimism, sickness began to appear, and it increased as worry and discouragement mounted. Later on I made many long, hard trips to the homestead country, usually without pay.

Failure of the grain crop the first year did not discourage the majority of the settlers; they did not expect much the first year. Failure of their gardens was a more serious handicap, as they expected to raise garden truck to live on and expected to can enough for the winter. Many hauled water for several miles for their gardens only to have the frost ruin them. Canned vegetables in the stores were expensive because of the long freight haul from the railroad. The prospect of having to buy canned vegetables at the stores made the settlers' remaining capital look much smaller.

The high price of chicken feed that had to be freighted into the country made it necessary for the chickens to forage at large, and the abundance of coyotes, badgers, skunks, bob cats, eagles, hawks and owls made chicken raising difficult. Conditions were not favorable for keeping dairy cows, and no hogs were raised as there was no forage for them. Although the antelope were protected by law, they furnished considerable meat to the settlers for a time, but they were soon scarce, very wild, and hard to get. The sage hens were being rapidly killed off. With the appearance of more and more automobiles in the cities, the price of horses began to slump, and some of the hungry settlers occasionally killed an unbranded range horse or colt, but that was still risky. The jack rabbit was the first pest and last resort. Many a jack rabbit was killed for food when provisions were low, although they were not considered fit to eat by most people.

After the second crop failure, some of the wiser settlers began to leave the country. There were many however who were determined to stay the necessary five years and prove up on their land, and persisted in trying to make the land produce a crop of grain. When money gave out, the head of the family often went to town and got work in order to buy provisions, leaving his family to work on the homestead. Very often the wife and children remained to plow, grub sagebrush, haul wood and water, and do the work of a man.

The courage and pluck of that little family, fighting a losing battle against insurmountable difficulties, were inspiring. They were people who would fight to the last without complaint, and blame no one if they lost. There were many others like them in the homestead country, the sort of people who have formed the foundation and backbone of our American civilization. Nowhere else have I seen such exemplification of the brotherhood of man as I witnessed in the homestead country. Everyone was always ready and willing to help his neighbor, or anyone whose condition was worse than his own, without expecting any compensation, even if it exhausted his last resource.

I was often called to see sick homesteaders who needed proper food more than medicine, and was often out my time, livery hire, and the money I gave them to buy food. The majority of them fought to the last ditch, but the time finally came when they had to surrender and leave the country.

Many honest, hard-working people lost years of their time at the hard labor, and all their capital, trying to make farms out of land that was entirely unsuited for it. Thousands of acres of the finest range were ruined, for when the sagebrush and bunch grass were cleared off, and the land plowed, the wind blew enough of the top soil away so that the bunch grass would not grow again. All because the officials in Washington, who knew nothing about the country, thought it was suitable for dry farming and would not listen to the advice of the old settlers who knew what they were talking about.[35]

By World War I, the homestead era on the desert lands of Central Oregon was virtually over. Homesteaders' cabins quickly fell into disrepair. Wind overturned some of the buildings. Fences became broken and gates hung limply on

Lands on the High Desert offered by a Bend realtor. This photo was taken on Bond Street about 1913 at the height of homesteading. (Phil F. Brogan photo)

Photo taken about 1915 in Bend, at the corner of Wall Street and Oregon Avenue, shows the first motorized truck that used the Bend-Burns highway. Lara's store is where J.C. Penney is now located. (Phil F. Brogan photo)

Left: Close-up photo reveals details of construction of Glenn Cabin—lodgepole pine logs sealed with mud and well-built window casings. Right: One clue to the date of occupancy of Glenn Cabin is "reading the wallpaper." Entryway to the cabin is decorated by January 15, 1922, edition of the *Sunday Oregonian*. (Kathy Bowman photos)

All that remains of the roof of Glenn Cabin are the thin lodgepole roof supports and a scattering of shingles. Smoke-darkened guide for the stovepipe gives testimony to the importance of wood fires for heating homesteaders' cabins. (Kathy Bowman photo) sagging hinges. In later years, the automobile provided better access to the desert from urban areas of Oregon. Curiosity seekers, souvenir hunters and vandals hastened the destruction of scattered homesteads.

Here and there, throughout the desert, the determined traveler can still come across visible reminders from half a century ago. The following description, composed in August, 1976, vividly portrays a nostalgic landscape:

Many remnants of early settlements are scattered across the desert landscape of Central Oregon. Farms and ranches once were numerous during the early homesteading days. The buildings resulting from the efforts of settlers to make a living on the desert often gained a second function after their abandonment—they became silent monuments to an era. Old shacks or cabins and their accompanying corrals and sheds once busy with agricultural commerce now remain as silent markers, sometimes graced by the small flowers of domestic shrubs gone wild in the shelter of an east-facing wall.

Bouncing across the dusty hot road through a gently rolling rangeland of high sage and low bunchgrass, you look toward the steep ridges topped with juniper to discover Glenn Cabin, now a greying collection of abandoned corrals, living quarters and sheds nestled at the base of the hills. While many of these remnants of the past have fallen down, Glenn Cabin—which sits a little removed from one of the many bumpy, gate-crossed roads that traverse the BLM-managed grazing lands between Christmas Valley and Brothers—is one of the few that remain, evading the vandalisms of time and man.

This composite homestead was initially constructed of whole, slim lodgepole logs, carefully chinked with mud. Later a larger room was added on to the original homestead by hammering into place rough-sawn boards of inch-thick lumber. Great distances and dusty roads have not freed the ranch buildings from the effects of time and change of use, however. One wall of the built-on section of the cabin has been removed, allowing cattle to shelter within during extremes of desert weather. All the old furnishings are of course gone, but some reminders of the past survive. Still-legible advertising from a January 1922 edition of the *Sunday Oregonian* smoothly papers the walls of the narrow, offset entryway of the "new" part of the house. Special bargains on player pianos are hawked, while entreaties to become "high-powered salesmen" lure the young ranch hands to life in the big city of Portland.

Though a weathered greyness is apparent even in the most recent portion of Glenn Cabin, the inch-thick boards remain sturdy and straight. The walls of the older log-cabin part of the house have stayed strong also, but the skinny poles used to construct the roof over this room are warped and cracking, while the shingles that once covered them are nearly gone. In the time-shattered roof, a scorched guide for the stovepipe remains, blackened by the heat of many fires in a long-missing stove. Well-built, thick window casings pierce the log walls of the cabin. These had provided the former occupants with a vantage point from which to peer out toward the road to identify the occasional visitor riding horseback across the gently sloping desert.

People once crowded into these two tiny rooms to work, eat and sleep. Even two rooms could not afford the space for all the activities a ranch home must contain, so auxiliary structures were built. These ranged from a lean-to for storage to what may have been the smokehouse, complete with stacked walls of native stone. Today this collection of small accessory buildings near the main house has partially fallen down, the poles and posts used to construct them leaning and lying at crazy angles. A solitary spider weaving a simple web has become the lone user of these buildings now.

Not far away stood the many pens and corrals needed on an active ranch. Some, still standing, were made of tightly stacked posts, while others, once strong, have yielded to the harsh desert elements and now half-stand, half-lie in their places. Close at hand is a short, shallow trench lined with rocks where brands once glowed in the fire when the sweaty, dusty work of branding calves had to be done.

Scattered around the deserted headquarters of this once busy ranch are dark cast-iron field implements and weatherworn feed troughs, symbols of man's attempt to find a place in the harsh, beautiful land of the Central Oregon desert country.[36]

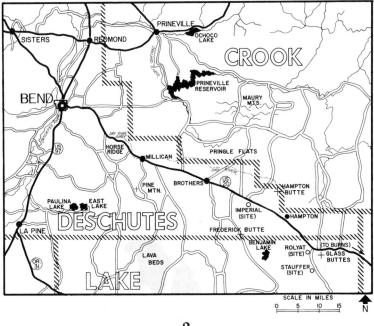

3

ALONG THE BEND-BURNS HIGHWAY

A one-day trip from Bend will easily enable motorists to get a feeling for the main desert features discussed in this section. Further exploration on other visits can provide opportunities to discover additional features that have historical, geological, or scenic interests. But the fast-moving motorist will find little to excite his curiosity as he travels this road. Mile after mile of sagebrush is interrupted only by rimrock and rolling hills, save for an occasional abandoned homestead.

Tedious as the journey between Bend and Burns may seem today, consider how the journey was by auto stage in 1913:

The desert was entirely new to me; so was the desert automobile. I had been looking forward eagerly to this first sight of the sage plains; but I had not expected the automobile, and

43

could see nothing whatever of the sagebrush until I had learned to ride the car. I had ridden an automobile before; I had driven one, a staid and even-going Eastern car, which I had left at home in the stable. I thought I knew an automobile; but I found that I had never been on one of the Western desert breed. The best bucker at the Pendleton Round-up is but a rocking-horse in comparison. I doubt if you could experience death in any part of the world more times for twenty dollars than by auto-stage from Bend to Burns.

The trail takes account of every possible bunch of sagebrush and greasewood to be met with on the way. It never goes over a bunch if it can go around a bunch; and as there is nothing but bunches all the way, the road is very devious. It turns, here and there, every four or five feet (perhaps the sagebrush clumps average five feet apart), and it has a habit, too, whenever it sees the homesteader's wire fences, of dashing for them, down one side of the claim, steering clear of all the clumps of sage, but ripping along horribly near to the sizzling barbs of the wire and the untrimmed stubs on the juniper posts; then darting into the brush, this way, that way, every way, which in the end proves to be the way to Burns, but no one at the beginning of the trip could believe it—no one from the East, I mean.

The utter nowhereness of that desert trail! Of its very start and finish! I had been used to starting from Hingham and arriving—and I am two whole miles from the station at that. Here at Mullein Hill [in Boston] I can see South, East, and North Weymouth, plain Weymouth, and Weymouth Heights, with Queen Anne's Corner only a mile away; Hanover, Four Corners, Assinippi, Egypt, Cohasset, and Nantasket are hardly five miles off; and Boston itself is but sixty minutes distant by automobile, Eastern time.

It is not so between Bend and Burns. Time and space are a different concept there. Here in Hingham you are never without the impression of somewhere. If you stop you are in Hingham; if you go you are in Cohasset, perhaps. You are always somewhere. But between Bend and Burns you are always in the sagebrush and right on the distant edge of time, and space, as Kant and Schopenhauer maintained, are not world elements independent of myself, at all, but only *a priori* forms of per-

ceiving. That will not do from Bend to Burns. They are independent things out there. You can whittle them and shovel
them. They are sagebrush and sand, respectively. . . .

That, however, does not describe the journey; there was
plenty of change in that, at the rate we went, and according to
the exceeding great number of sagebrushes we passed. It was
all change; through all sage. We never really tarried by the side
of any sagebrush. It was impossible to do that and keep the car
shying rhythmically—now on its two right wheels, now on its
two left wheels—past the sagebrush next ahead. Not the
journey, I say; it was only the concept, the impression of the
journey, that can be likened to Brahman. But that single, un-
mitigated impression of sage and sand, of nowhereness, was so
entirely unlike all former impressions that I am glad I made the
journey from Boston in order to go from Bend to Burns.

You lose no time getting at the impression. It begins in Bend
—long before, indeed, being distributed generally all over this
Oregon country. At Bend the railroad terminates. The only thing
you can do at Bend is to go back—unless you are bound for
Burns. The impression does not begin at Bend, and it does not
end at Burns. It only deepens. For at Burns there is not so
much as a railroad terminus. You cannot go back from Burns, or
"out," as the citizens say, until there are enough of your mind
to charter the auto-stage. The next railroad terminus to Burns is
at Vale, east-northeast one hundred and thirty-five miles of
sage beyond.

Not split by time and space, and free from all change, single,
deep, indelible, gray is the desert from Bend to Burns.

It was 7:10 in the morning when we started from Bend, it was
after eight in the evening when we swung into Burns. At noon
we halted for dinner at a rude road-house, half of the journey
done; at one o'clock we started on with a half of it yet to go—
at the same pace, over the same trail, through the same dust
and sun and sage, the other car of our party, that had followed
us so far, now taking the lead. There were details enough,
there was variety enough, had one but the time and the eyes to
see. I had neither. This was my first day in the desert; and it
was the desert that I wanted to traverse—it was the sage and
the sand, the roll, the reach to the horizon, the gray, sage gray,

that I had come out to see. I must travel swift and look far off. For you cannot compass the desert horizon at a glance. Nor can you see at a glance this desert gray, it is so low a tone, a color so hard to fix. I must see sage gray until it should dye the very grain of my imagination, as the bitter flavor of the sage strains the blood, and tastes in the very flesh of sage hen.

On we sped into the sage, on into the lengthening afternoon; the scattered juniper trees, strangely like orchard trees at a distance, becoming more numerous, the level stretches more varied and broken, with here and there a cone-like peak appearing—Glass Buttes to the south, Buck mountain to the north, with Wagontire and Iron Mountain farther off. Early in the forenoon we had passed several homesteaders' claims, spots of desolation in the desert, and now, as the afternoon wore on, the lonely settler's shack and wire fence began to appear again.[37]

The Highway to Millican

Sixty years ago a traveler along the Bend-Burns highway described the landscape as far as Millican:

One drives southeastward from Bend through miles of land that is mostly irrigated. Then without apparent change of altitude, so gradual is the ascent, and without once being out of sight of cultivated farms, he comes into the lower end of Millican Valley. This is the High Desert, where people have been telling me that nothing could be grown; and well as I know this country and long as I have been faithful to it, I expected to see nothing but sagebrush to the level and uninteresting horizon. When we topped a rise, swung around Horse Ridge, and I saw before me a checkerboard of rectangular stubble fields as far as the eye could reach, I stood up in the car, waved my hat, and shouted a wild hurrah for the brave homesteaders and this, their answer to the pessimists.[38]

Today, for a dozen miles along the Bend-Burns highway, use of water from irrigation canals and well water have contributed to the creation of a pleasant rural landscape with mini farms, residences, and alfalfa fields mixed in with natural sage and juniper; and the main highway to Millican no longer "swings" around Horse Ridge, although the old road is still there for the nostalgic traveler. The new, wide highway pierces the saddle of the ridge almost as straight as an arrow, skirting the southern rim of the Dry River Gorge. The red oil roadbed cut into the hillside to the south of the new highway is a legacy from a road built around 1930 and abandoned just a few years ago.

The "checkerboard of rectangular stubble fields," described above have disappeared, but the discerning eye can still detect the faint marks of rectangular fields. However, they show up more clearly on aerial photographs.

Millican Valley, a vast, flat expanse of sage and sand, lies ahead of the motorist cresting Horse Ridge. Pine Mountain secures the southern edge of the valley, and the smooth, time-worn slopes of Bear Creek Butte dominate the northern rim. Highway 20 slices across the valley floor, climbs the distant hills and disappears over the rim.

The Dry River

At one time during part of the Pleistocene time, Millican Valley was inundated by a vast lake. To the east of Millican Valley, separated by a lava ridge, a second lake held runoff from Hampton Butte. Today, two dry waterfalls, smoothed and polished by the rushing river, connect the two lakes. Evidence of the erosive power of the water in the streams is seen in the many potholes cut by the grinding of small rocks trapped in holes in the stream-bed lava. Sedimentary strata formed by the ancient lake show up along the highway at the eastern base of Horse Ridge. The lake was believed to have been formed thousands of years ago in a more humid climate than now. In recent times (February 1936) heavy rain sent a flood of brown water through the Dry River in the Whittaker Holes area, destroying a section of the Central Oregon Highway. West of Millican, miniature lakes formed in the channel of the ancient river. The water then disappeared into fissures or into the sand.

The Dry River was described in 1905 by Geologist I.C. Russell:

> Our first camp after leaving Button Spring was in the bed of an ancient stream known as Dry River, which at one time drained the Great Sandy Desert. The course of the channel is well marked from the west end of the desert to Deschutes River, a distance of over 50 miles. At our camp, about 6 miles east of Pauline Mountains [now Pine Mountain] the old river bed is a well-defined canyon, 30 to 40 feet deep and 150 feet wide, with walls of columnar basalt. About 12 miles farther west the canyon becomes deeper, and for a distance of 4 or 5 miles is a narrow defile with vertical walls of basalt. In the river bed at the time of our visit there was no water, but by digging in the sand that partly fills the channel a sufficient supply for camp purposes for a single day was obtained at a depth of 6 feet.[39]

Several branches of tributaries to the Dry River, as it is now known, can be seen from the air. A study of topographic maps reveals the course of the Dry River and the watercourse of its tributaries. The shoreline of the lake, it is believed, was near the present timberline of Pine Mountain.

An outlet for the lake was created to the north of Horse Ridge and, in time, the 300-foot-deep Dry River Gorge was carved by water flowing out of Lake Millican. The gorge can be approached either from the flat plain to the west or from a dirt road leading north off U.S. Highway 20 at the Millican Valley base of the Horse Ridge grade. A viewpoint from the north side of U.S. 20 at the Horse Ridge highway summit provides travelers with a fine vista of the Dry River Gorge and the Millican Valley. The geology of the Dry River and Lake Millican is explained on a large, wooden roadside marker at the highway summit.

In 1927, the discovery of traces of an Indian encampment in a small sandy area within the Dry River Gorge was reported in the Bend *Bulletin*. Over 200 different Indian paintings (pictographs), showing deer, antelope, lizards, snakes, and a rayed

Highway 20 slices through exposed sedimentary deposits from prehistoric Lake Millican.

Dry River Gorge, West of Millican, is a 300-foot chasm readily seen from a viewpoint on Highway 20.

PREHISTORIC RIVER

AGES AGO A RIVER FLOWED ACROSS THE HIGH DESERT COUNTRY IN THE ROCKY CANYON SEVERAL HUNDRED YARDS BEYOND THIS MARKER. THE PREHISTORIC RIVER DRAINED A LARGE ICE AGE LAKE THAT FORMED FROM THE BLOCKING OF NORMAL DRAINAGE IN THE AREA BY LAVA FLOWS. THE LAKE COVERED A LARGE AREA TO THE EAST IN THE VICINITY OF THE PRESENT MILLICAN COUNTRY.

DURING PERIODS OF HIGH WATER THE LAKE SPILLED OVER A LOW PASS AT THE EASTERN EDGE OF HORSE RIDGE—THE RIDGE SEEN BEHIND YOU AND TO YOUR RIGHT. THE ESCAPING WATER CUT INTO THE LOOSELY CONSOLIDATED LAVA FLOWS CREATING THE ROCKY GORGE VISIBLE FROM THE VIEWPOINT AND LATER CALLED DRY RIVER. ONCE FREE FROM THE HORSE RIDGE BARRIER DRY RIVER FLOWED NORTH INTO THE PRESENT CROOKED RIVER. EVIDENCE INDICATES THAT THE ANCIENT RIVER WAS ONCE THE SCENE OF MANY INDIAN ENCAMPMENTS NEAR ITS SOURCE AT THE LAKE.

State-of-Oregon marker at Dry River Gorge.

Indian pictographs on walls of Dry River Gorge. Over 200 different pictographs showing deer, antelope, lizards, etc., were indelibly painted in red and yellow pigments. (Oregon Historical Society photo)

50

sun, were indelibly painted in red and yellow pigments on a small area of columnar basaltic cliff within the gorge. Today, the paintings are quite difficult to detect as the marks of vandals have partially obscured the signs.

The history behind the Indian writings found at the Dry River site—tales of warfare in Central Oregon—was reported "tongue in cheek" in the Bend newspaper in 1927:

Pictures with mineral paints on walls of basalt in which Dry River long ages ago coursed northward through Central Oregon is a record of a battle between Indians and the story of the elevation of a warrior of the Elk clan to heights which approached that of a chieftain. This was learned here today when Nipo Strongheart, known as Chtu-Tem-Nah by the Confederated Tribes of the Yakima, read some of the groups of hieroglyphics which are scattered over approximately 200 yards of the eastern wall of Dry River, just west of Millican and some 28 miles east of Bend.

Dominating the great mass of Indian petrographs on the sunrise wall of the ancient river channel is the pictured record of a fighter who scalped or captured at least a score of opposing warriors of the Shoshone, or Snake tribe. Not only did this warrior of old Central Oregon picture his conquests, but he painted on the rock a challenge to any doubting his prowess.

After studying a group of pictures of the Yakima writings found in Dry River, Strongheart, grandson of a Yakima chief who fought against the advances of white men in the west, expressed his opinion that the entire group of paintings in Dry River deal with a battle—or a series of battles between Indian tribes many years ago.

The tribe which opposed the warrior who made a record of the expedition in hieroglyphics was, evidently, the Shoshones, known generally in this part of the state as the Snakes, it is the opinion of Strongheart. Some of the petroglyphs indicate that the tribes which left the record were the Bannocks. The Snakes and the Bannocks probably met in the plateau country east of the Deschutes and fought. Unless the story of this war as pictured on the rocks is biased, the group encamped in the bed of Dry River was the victor, Strongheart reads from the writings.[40]

Directly under the writings and buried under two feet of drifted sand, hundreds of arrowheads have been recovered. Old campfires had been raked over and yellow teeth of deer, antelopes, beavers, and coyotes found. Seashells were discovered in the burned remnants of the ancient campfires, possibly proving that at least one migrating tribe had camped there. The fact that the arrowheads were of chipped obsidian (black volcanic glass) indicates that the tribes obtained materials for their spears, arrows, skinning knives, and needles from at least as far away as Newberry Crater.

Other Indian campsites and pictographs have been located elsewhere in the old sand-choked river channel which meanders across the Central Oregon desert. Sketched on the canyon walls are symbols possibly depicting fish. Fossil bones of fish have been discovered in road cuts in the desert area where Lake Millican once covered the lake basin. It may never be known for sure whether Indians fished in Lake Millican or near the interconnecting falls but evidence points to that possibility.

Homesteading Millican Valley

Early in the twentieth century the agricultural potential of the Millican Valley was noted and described:

The High Desert is a scope of country whose possibilities as a farming and stock country are now little known. Bunch grass stands on it today knee high and it is believed that it will prove wonderfully productive when placed under irrigation and will develop into a great wheat country unsurpassed by any in the northwest.[41] . . . The land is level, free from stones and the soil, for the most part deep, producing a good crop of sagebrush.[42]

The settlement of Millican took its name from George Millican, an early-day stockman of Central Oregon who made his first trip into this part of the state from the McKenzie River in 1863. Cattle were brought into the Crooked River country in 1868 and later located on a ranch in the Millican Valley. The original plans called for the post office of the newly formed desert community to be

Right: George Millican homestead about 1915, looking north. (Phil Brogan photo) Left: Millican area, drilling for water, 1916. (USFS photo)

George Millican homestead about 1915. The corral and windmill were located in the dry River Gorge. (Phil Brogan photo)

Millican homestead site in 1977, taken from the same location as the 1915 photo.

The "town" of Millican, all of it, serves motorists traveling Highway 20 between Bend and Burns.

named Mt. Pine, after nearby Pine Mountain. However, Mt. Pine sounded too much like La Pine, also located in Central Oregon, so the Mt. Pine name was rejected by postal authorities in Washington, D.C.

Irrigation waters for the High Desert were planned to come from Paulina Lake. Indeed there were several different plans for using waters from East and Paulina lakes for irrigating areas extending from Millican Valley to Fort Rock Valley. Lack of irrigation water notwithstanding, homesteading in the Millican area proceeded. Weekly reports from many newly established settlements on the Central Oregon desert were received by the *Bulletin:*

Nine teams left the Wenandy Barn all loaded with lumber for homesteaders who are building in the neighborhood of the Millican Ranch, 30 miles southeast of Bend. It is understood that practically every desirable area has been taken up by settlers, who are now moving onto their 320 acre ranches and making improvements.[43]

A cautious 1912 report included the following description:

The cabins of settlers are seen dotting the broad valley, with a few acres cleared and put in cultivation. This valley has been settled up in only a little over a year and hence there has not been time for making extensive improvements.[44]

Improvements were made and work on the homesteads in the Millican Valley continued. In 1912, the need for erecting a school was seen and a site selected. A that time, forty homesteads, with fifteen children, were in the Millican Valley. By March, 1913, the boundaries for a school district were defined and the school site chosen (section 6, township 20 south, range 15 east).

For several years reports from the Millican Valley to the Bend newspaper were quite optimistic.

In the spring of 1916, a shipment of 2600 fruit and nut trees was made to Charles Hartwig. About 75 acres were planted with apple, peach, pear, plum, nut and other trees. Experiments with alfalfa and flax were very successful. Although in early July a report from Millican stated that the young orchards were doing well, there appeared to be no further progress reports on the trees.

The valley landscape, in 1977 almost devoid of human habitation, was certainly undergoing changes by 1913:

> One team of horses plowed ten acres of ground in four days last week. Others cleared sagebrush and planted rye. A good flow of water in the old river bed has been found at a depth of only five feet. A homesteader at Horse Ridge is erecting a store at milepost 23 and expects to open for business in the near future.[45]

By mid-1913 it was reported:

> The entire valley is dotted with the cabins of those who have come to stay. In the neighborhood of sixty homesteaders were located and more claims were filed this year. 500 acres are cleared of sagebrush and put in cultivation, principally rye and wheat.[46]

In 1915, a demonstration farm, with ten acres planted in marcus wheat, was established. That same year, a Millican Homesteaders' Development Association was formed to help promote the settlement of the valley. The following year, the name of the development association was changed to Mt. Pine Boosters.

The Millican school, by late 1915, had nineteen children in attendance. School reports indicate that both enrollments and attendance figures fluctuated widely from month to month. Eventually, as crops failed and homesteaders abandoned their claims and the flu epidemic raged (1918), the school lost most of its pupils. In late December, 1922, only four pupils were enrolled. By then, the valley landscape had already experienced a deteriorating change.

In 1930, the Central Oregon highway bypassed Millican when the road was rerouted from around the southern base of Horse Ridge to be realigned over the ridge. The "town" of Millican was then moved half a mile to the north to a location near the Dry River bed. The original site of Millican had been the P.B. Johnson home-

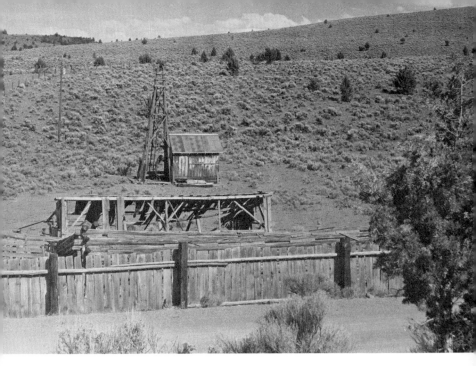

Juniper lands and an abandoned well and corral as seen from the gravel road between Millican and Pine Mountain.

Elevation and increased precipitation, especially winter snows on Pine Mountain, make possible the transition from desert (as at Millican) to Ponderosa-pine forest as shown above. Pine Mountain was the picnic site for early-day homesteaders living in the Millican Valley.

Pine Mountain as seen across the Millican Valley.

Pine Mountain. The 6,595-foot elevation is home to the University of Oregon Astronomical Observatory.

stead filed in 1912, when Johnson had found water at 390 feet after drilling through lava strata and conglomerate.

For years Millican was the only "town" in Oregon which had a population of one person, yet appeared on maps. In recent times, the whole "town"—one lonely gas station with a general store complete with an array of outbuildings—has been on the real-estate market.

Pine Mountain

Rising out of the sagebrush plain like an island, Pine Mountain (formerly Pauline Mountains) is a dominant landscape feature south of the Millican Valley. Because of its elevation above the desert, the mountain receives sufficient moisture for the growth of juniper and Ponderosa pine on its high, northern flanks. Russell, in distinguishing Pauline Mountains from the Paulinas and describing the geology and the extensive views from the mountain, stated:

The name Pauline Mountains is used on the General Land Office map of Oregon to designate a prominent group of hills situated 42 miles directly south of Prineville and approximately in the geographic center of the State. Locally, however, the same name is also applied to other equally conspicuous elevations in the vicinity of Pauline and East lakes. Although these two groups of picturesque hills or mountains are connected by a tract of high land, they are independent, so far as their geologic histories are concerned, and as they will no doubt receive much attention from geologists and others in the future, it is thought advisable to designate them by separate names. . . .

The Pauline Mountains proper rise boldly from the bordering basaltic plain to a height of about 1,500 feet. The main summit is a sharp ridge trending N. 70 degrees E. (magnetic), which at each end curves abruptly southward, so as to partly inclose an amphitheater nearly 2 miles in diameter. The rock along the crest of the ridge and forming the conspicuous pinnacles rising from it is a hard, purplish material resembling quartzite, but from field observations simply is believed to be mainly a consolidated rhyolithic tuff. The sides of the mountain are thickly covered with quartz sand. The stratification of the rock is well defined and the dip on the crest of the main ridge is downward to the east at an angle of about 16 degrees, the strike being at right angles to the trend of the ridge.

In the curved western portion of the ridge, and exposed in the west wall of the great amphitheater, the dip is south at an angle of from 16 degrees to 17 degrees. The mountain is thus shown to be an eroded remnant of what was probably at one time a great volcanic cone older than the surrounding basalt, but no fossils were discovered by means of which its age might be determined. To the northwest of the main ridge and about half a mile distant rises an outstanding butte composed of rock of the same character as the main elevation, left in bold relief by erosion.

The floor of the amphitheater on the south side of the Pauline Mountains is deeply covered, over an area of 3 or 4 square miles, with nearly white pumiceous lapilli, which the wind has drifted into dunes. This barren area is bordered on the south by an open forest of junipers. The mountain itself, more especially its northern slope, bears groves of yellow pine and has a well-defined forest about its western base.

The view from the topmost pinnacle of Pauline Mountains is far-reaching and superb. In the east, beyond the barren yellow plain of the Great Sandy Desert, Hampton and Glass buttes are in plain sight, and the tapering summit of Placidia Butte can be recognized in the blue distance. To the south, in the vicinity of Button Spring, about 50 recent volcanic craters can be counted, and in the western sky rise the snow-clad summits of several of the great peaks that dominate the generally even crest line of the Cascade Mountains.[47]

Long ago, during the homesteading days, settlers living in the valley used Pine Mountain for summer picnics. In January, 1967, plans were laid for installing an astronomical observatory housing a 24-inch telescope on the summit of Pine Mountain. The observatory was placed in operation August 4, 1967, under cloudless skies with near perfect viewing conditions.

The clear, dry desert air of Central Oregon—a contrast to the often hazy atmospheric conditions found west of the Cascades in the Willamette Valley—was an important factor when Dr. E.G. Ebbighausen, of the University of Oregon, selected Pine

Mountain as the site of the observatory. The observatory has contributed significantly to astronomical knowledge but, at times, limited financing has jeopardized its operations. (Much of the work of the 24-inch telescope has been devoted to study of binary star systems in Cygnus, where evidence of a mysterious "black hole" was found.) Visitors are permitted at the observatory but should check hours with the Bend Chamber of Commerce before venturing the 25 miles to Millican plus a nine-mile climb on a gravel road from Millican to the 6595-foot summit.

At times during the winter, snows of several feet isolate the resident caretakers at the Pine Mountain Observatory; contact with the outside world is then limited to the telephone. A large stock of essentials—including a 16,000-gallon water supply, plenty of books, and cross-country skis—help the caretakers through the winter.

Brothers

About fifteen miles east of Millican on the windswept desert, and straddling Highway 20, is the isolated town of Brothers. The name of the town has been traced to "several fraternal family groups that settled in the area, of whom various Stenkamp brothers comprised one of more notable."[48]

The setting of Brothers, its economy and lifestyle are familiar to those who have traveled the Bend-Burns Highway and taken time to pause at the State of Oregon rest area or at the Brothers' Store:

Brothers is as closely knit as the name indicates. The tiny cluster of buildings is perched on a rolling ridge and commands sweeping views in all directions—the dignified bluish peak of Hampton Butte to the east and the white-capped Cascades to the west. Higher ridges surrounding the old lake basin frame the north and south edges.

The town is split by Highway 20 which provides the lifeblood of the community. It supplies labor for the highway crews in the pale green government houses. These are part of the first compartment of Brothers—the neat homes of regulation color, a few mobile homes and a wooden warehouse surmounted by an official light that dominates the nightscape. Across the highway is lush green lawn with small picnic areas.

Another compartment of the Brothers nucleus is the old whitewashed, cement-walled store, a strange blend of the old and new. Outside are gas pumps, tow trucks and the tools of a modern auto mechanic, yet by the door to the cafe is an old-time, "crank-'em-up" telephone. Behind the highway-fronting store a rutted road in a horse pasture serves as a landing field. Next to this old-new mix, a modern mobile home stands, too new to show the inevitable aging of the desert.

Nearby is the school area—a hodgepodge of single structures—a one-room red schoolhouse, a shiny barn-like tin auditorium, and a mobile home for the one teacher are crowded against the highway, leaving the other half of the school lands as a barren, level playfield.

The highway keeps Brothers functioning and alive. It brings the children to school. It is the livelihood of the road crews and provides tourist trade for the local store. [49]

Brothers is located on an extensive northwest-trending fault zone which bears the same name as the community. This fault is "part of the northwesterly portion of the Oregon-Nevada lineament which reaches from Mount Jefferson in Oregon southeastward into north-central Nevada. Normal faults of the zone and the many volcanic vents along the zone represent only the surface manifestations of deformation on a large, deeply buried structure, the exact nature of which is not known." [50] It is these linear faults that have created many of the rimrocks which are prominent features of the desert landscape.

Pringle Flats

Pringle Flats is, or rather was, a little-known homestead community located a dozen or so miles northeast of Brothers. The ghostly remnants of cabins are still to be found, either conspicuously rising above the flat sagebrush plain or partially obscured by juniper trees in the sheltered foothills bordering the desert country.

The small wooden schoolhouse at Brothers. The one teacher resides in the
mobile home (left).

The Brothers Store, with cafe, gas station and post office, serves residents of the area and
travelers pausing on their journey along Highway 20.

Typical rimrock and desert scenery north of Brothers.

Pringle Flats social hall—scene of community gatherings on the High Desert. Pringle Flats, once called Warm Springs, had no post office or store but supported a school which served homesteaders' children.

64

Homestead claims were filed in the area in 1911. However, stockmen had grazed livestock in the region as early as 1873. At that time, Pringle Flats had been known as Warm Springs, because of the heated waters which boiled up from the ground and which were used by thousands of livestock year-round.

By the summer of 1912, homesteaders at Pringle Flats were having success with growing grains, principally rye and hardy vegetables such as lettuce, radishes and beets. A school district was formed in 1912 and immediately served a dozen children of settlers, most of whom were Americans of German descent from Washington State. Pringle Flats—named for O.C. Pringle, an early settler—never had a store or a post office. Mail came twice a week from Prineville to the post office at Held, in the Maury Mountains to the north.

By 1915, the school enrollment had reached 37. The 1915 Fourth of July celebrations at Pringle Flats attracted 250 people who participated in or watched horse and foot races and wrestling matches. A large social hall served the residents in the Pringle Flats region for many years. Even after the homesteaders on the desert had yielded to the aridity of the climate, ranchers living in the better-watered hill country still congregated for square dances and socials at the Pringle Flats hall.

The landscape of Pringle Flats today tells the history of the area. The schoolhouse has long since been moved. The dance hall remains—silent and empty. Several isolated homesteaders' cabins, in various states of disrepair, are still to be seen. Wind-blown sand is gradually hiding attempts at dry farming, or covering the rusting metal of farm machinery which was left behind. Windmills have long ceased to pump water and now groan and creak eerily in the desert winds. Although Pringle Flats is one of the lesser-known desert communities, its landscape still visibly reflects all the hopes and failures of the homesteaders.

Imperial

East of Brothers, the straight desert highway traverses the bed of a prehistoric dry lake, whose geology and landscape inspired a 1937 *Bulletin* editorial by Phil Brogan, author of *East of the Cascades:*

THE DESERT'S STORY

Members of the Bend delegation who drove to Burns recently for the conference with Governor Charles H. Martin and his highway commission found the so-called high desert, across juniper-covered hills and sage plateaus, in an unusual setting. Light rain was falling above the 4,000-foot level; low, dark clouds just grazed the high summits of Pine mountain, Hampton and Glass Buttes, and over the vast region, reaching to a distance of 70 miles, was a strange coloring. Under the rain clouds, the subdued coloring brought into striking relief topographical details that gave a clue to the ancient history of the region.

Under the customary glaring light of the high plateau, the desert generally hides away its old secrets, guarding them as treasures of ages that reach into that primeval past when semitropical forests covered the Hampton highlands. But such is not the case when dark clouds drift over the region. Elevations scarcely noticed in brilliant light come into view, old lava flows whose margins have been eroded by the storms of centuries are noticeable and vast depressions once occupied by huge lakes are brought into relief.

One of the most striking of these old lake beds is in the vicinity of Hampton, and members of the Bend group who made the recent trip to Burns under the heavy storm clouds were amazed to discover that even the shorelines of Lake Hampton were visible and that a nearly perpendicular rim of basalt to the northeast graphically told the story of the manner in which the ancient lake came into existence: A great earth fault developed, and the old drainage system was blocked by the rock barrier, and runoff from the Hampton uplift filled the depression to a depth of probably 60 feet. Lake Hampton, on whose ancient western shoreline the ghost town of Imperial stood some 20 years ago, was probably 20 miles long in its flush days. It disappeared long ago, probably when the vast lakes of south-central Oregon started shrinking.

The full-light of rainy days on the generally dry plateau also distinctly outlines the vents of old volcanoes—thundering cones

Water is one of the most precious resources of the desert. Photo, taken in Pringle Flats country, shows well (windmill now missing), concrete tank and water trough cut out of tree trunk.

Windblown sand hides part of farm equipment left by homesteader.

Solitary windmill is the only standing remnant of the homestead town of Imperial, two miles south of Highway 20. Hampton Butte is in background.

Highway 20 slices through sagebrush and sand where former Lake Hampton once flooded the valley. Snow-clad hills in background are Hampton Butte.

of the remote past from which lava flowed to build the midstate highlands and cover for eternity the underlying sedimentary formations that hold records of sequoia forests.

There are some who consider the high desert a detriment to travel across Central Oregon. That desert, once its strange story is known, may prove an asset, just as the barren wastes of the southwest are now attracting thousands of motorists each season.[51]

In 1938, the Oregon State Highway Department, while constructing a new highway across the prehistoric lake bed, saved several thousand dollars by using the rock that was broken up and partly rounded by waves of the Pleistocene lake.

About ten miles east of Brothers and south of the highway, a conspicuous metal windmill stands alone on the sagebrush plains. This marks the site of Imperial. Imperial does not even qualify as a ghost town today, but at one time, it was a "busy desert village, with one main street boasting two stores, several residences and businesses, a school, a dance hall, a blacksmith shop, a well and a windmill and post office, which served scores of desert homesteaders."

At the 1914 Fourth of July celebration at Imperial, "150 people gathered to participate in foot and horse races, a bucking contest and claims to the most popular lady and most handsome man. A barbecued beef and mutton dinner was served and was pronounced delicious."[52]

Imperial was widely and falsely advertised by realtors. The Bend newspaper frequently carried a detailed advertisement with a description that fit the Imperial area—though the name was not used. Prospective homesteaders were lured by statements touting, "The New Klondike of the West in an attractive valley, 35 to 75 miles beyond Bend, a valley originally a large inland lake which has been filled up with the erosion of sediment from its surrounding hills and mountains." The soil was described as being "15 to 20 feet deep and consisting of rich, sandy loam mixed with a sufficient blending of volcanic ash from the Cascade Mountains and extinct volcanoes to make it extremely fertile, as indicated by the enormous growth of sagebrush and bunch grass." [53]

Also mentioned in the promoters' ad was the climate (320 days of sunshine a year; 12-18" rainfall), the availability of fuel and building material from the surrounding hills and the excellent big-game hunting—bear, elk, deer. Agriculture in the valley was described as being dry-land farming, the same as in the fertile Palouse country of eastern Washington. Travel details and costs of getting to Bend—where prospective purchasers of land would be met and shown the valley—were included in the advertisement.

Imperial was well publicized outside Oregon. Cardboard posters 3-1/2 feet wide and 6 feet long were mounted in prominent places on the walls of passenger-station waiting rooms throughout the United States. A promoter from the Imperial Valley of California, attempting to lure people to Central Oregon, boasted of the future of great cities of the Northwest—Imperial, Portland and Seattle. "Millions of acres of open government land in the Palouse Region of Oregon yield 60-bushel wheat crops and have not experienced crop failures." [54]

W.A. Rockie—a former soil conservationist at Portland, Oregon—was a teen-ager in 1906 when he mounted 30 of the posters in the waiting rooms in 30 towns in eastern Nebraska. In 1918, while classifying public domain in Central Oregon, he inspected an abandoned homestead and found, nailed over a broken window in an empty cabin, a dirty and torn cardboard poster identical to those he had placed in Nebraska.

Lots in Imperial were "sold" throughout the United States, even long after Imperial had faded and disappeared. As recently as 1965, Crook and Deschutes County officials still received letters from people who had purchased lots seeking information on population and on the progress of irrigation systems. However, back in 1918, Imperial and other homestead communities on the High Desert encountered many problems, one of which was the shortage of rye seed. This was practically the only grain that could be grown on the dry lands, and the previous year's crop had been a failure. The *Bulletin* stated:

Many homesteads are being abandoned for the season. A leave of absence is granted those who have not yet proved upon their claims, while others who have made final proof are selling out their holdings and going to work in the spruce and fir woods and shipyards on the coast. So great has been the exodus on the High Desert, that it has been found advisable to discontinue the post office at Imperial—where there were 125 residents in the vicinity, about five remain. Conditions are not as bad as in some other places, but the greater number of settlers' shacks have been closed up.[55]

For many homestead settlements on the Oregon High desert, this was the end of their existence. On the author's visit to Imperial in 1976, the silence of the desert around the site was broken only by a haunting wind moving over the sage, brushing the old windmill blade and causing it to creak and groan. A clearing under the windmill revealed a dry well, a scattering of bleached lumber and pieces of rusting iron. There was little to indicate what the landscape of Imperial was like sixty years ago.

Hampton Valley

The Hampton Valley area is the end of our desert travels along Highway 20. Beyond Glass Buttes, we are out of our Central Oregon region. For many years, several small pioneer communities in the Hampton Valley area sent weekly or periodic reports to the Bend newspaper.

Its bleak landscape was described by I.C. Russell earlier in this century. He mentions the deeply stream-sculptured mountains of Glass Buttes and Hampton Butte, rising approximately 1500 feet above the adjacent plains. There were groves of pines on the shaded northern slopes, but for the most part all was sagebrush and bunch grass. Russell wrote:

The few watering places, separated by wide intervals, in the surrounding country are well known to the residents of the region, and can readily be found by the stranger by following the well-beaten trails, but one might travel in a straight line almost any direction from the buttes [Glass] for distances of 40

Until lumber was available, homesteaders lived in tents at Stauffer. This photo, taken in the spring of 1912 (with snow still on ground), shows the rugged life for desert settlers. (Association of Oregon Geographers photo)

An abandoned homestead nestled at the base of Glass Buttes.

or more miles without discovering a flowing stream or a spring. So desolate is the country and so widely scattered are the few places where water can be had that even experienced "cowboys" in attempting to traverse it have in some instances become lost during storms and have nearly perished from thirst . . . .[56]

There are some cabins about the butte [Hampton], all occupied by energetic and most hospitable ranchers. The watering places have been enclosed by fences, and small areas about the lower slope of the butte are irrigated and produce good hay crops and some wheat. The value of the butte and the region about it, however, lies solely in its excellent pastures, its usefulness as a stock range being due largely to the fact that it is an outpost of industry in a generally waterless land. To the south the great desert, which in winter furnishes abundant pasturage, extends without a resident for 40 or more miles, while the butte itself is so thinly settled and the extent of the uninhabited country about it so vast that it is still almost in a state of nature. Its grasses are still luxuriant, and deer and antelope continue to make it their home; mountain sheep were formerly abundant, but have now vanished.

The remoteness of Hampton Butte from all commercial centers, the abundance of grass on its hills and vales, the number of its cool refreshing springs, the beauty of its groves of whispering pines and junipers, and perhaps more than all, the almost continuous sunshine that bathes its breezy slopes, make it wonderfully attractive to the traveler, from whatever land he may have wandered. As a health resort and a place of rest and recreation, it has but few rivals.[57]

Glass Buttes, elevation 6385 feet, which marks the eastern "border" of our region, is a prominent ancient volcano rising sharply above the desert plain. Rockhounds are well acquainted with it, and its reputation for fine specimens of obsidian is well deserved. Indeed, much of the desert sand to the south of the buttes is littered with shining black obsidian. Piles of obsidian found at adjacent abandoned homesteads in the Stauffer area (described below) indicate that early-day settlers, or their children, were also "rock hounds." The beauty of the obsidian found here prompted a *Bulletin* editorial titled "Imprisoned Sunsets":

Out in the Stauffer country of Central Oregon, where the Glass Butte formation dominates a vast plateau, there was recently discovered by chance a peculiar type of obsidian holding imprisoned all the colors of the rainbow. To this newly discovered volcanic glass, unknown in any other part of the world, has been given the name iridescent obsidian. The beautiful rock, each piece a gem in itself, was brought to the attention of Oregon mineral experts and collectors by P.L. Forbes and already the discovery has received mention in publications of nation-wide circulation.

The rainbow-like play of interference colors, distinctly visible in the peculiar obsidian, has mystified students of rare and semi-precious stones, and several theories have been advanced in explanation. Some geologists are of the opinion that the obsidian was hurled into the air through volcanic action and when still in a plastic state struck the ground. The impact, it is believed, might have disarranged the crystals, resulting in the strange and spectacular play of colors. Others believe that the volcanic glass bombs fell in water.

But regardless of the cause of the iridescence, the new type of obsidian is a strange rock, one which will probably attract much attention to the interesting volcanic formations in the plateau area to the east of Bend. Mr. Forbes is authority for the statement that in the Stauffer region have been found seven types of obsidian—and in proof of his statement he has brought to Bend pieces of rock which break the rays of the sun into a play of brilliant colors, and other bits of volcanic glass with a disappearing sheen of silver. One of the obsidian types is opaque and banded, with layers of blue, green, red, pink, and, among other mixed colors, gold. The golden variety of obsidian found in the Glass Butte area by Mr. Forbes is peculiar, having a delicate finely banded pattern of red and black material, but showing a play of golden colors. When properly cut, this type is just as attractive as gems from far countries.

A large amount of obsidian holding minute bubbles, probably formed by air or gases, is also found in the Stauffer region. Of this variety, a small quantity has been found which exhibits the bubbles in a minute form, as sort of a haze. When cut and polished, this rock has a distinct sheen, not unlike that of moonstone.

Out in the Glass Butte terrain, Mr. Forbes has also discovered a few specimens of common and iridescent obsidian mixed, probably due to a molten bomb falling on another liquid mass. Although the theory has been advanced in explanation of iridescent obsidian that molten glass was thrown from a crater with great force and was partly crystalized, we have a theory of our own to account for the strange interplay of rainbow colors.

We believe that long ages ago the cooling volcanic magmas, high on Glass Butte, caught and imprisoned the colors of a Central Oregon sun. [58]

Hampton Valley, like the Millican Valley country, was homesteaded around 1910. The story of the optimism, then the failure, was similar:

W.P. Ireland now has the satisfaction of witnessing the transforming into ranches of the entire range country. All of the Ireland Valley, south of Hampton Butte, has been taken up by homesteaders who are now moving in. The land is practically level, free from stones, with deep soil, rich bunch grass and sage and plenty of water.

A score of houses are in the course of construction, a dozen built, fences going up, and land being plowed and put into crops. Mr. Ireland says his well is full and despite its constant use showed no signs of being unable to meet the demands upon it. Many other wells are being dug. Oats are being planted, spring rye has a splendid start and some wheat will be put in soon. Before the year is past he expects to see heavy shipments of wheat from the district. Hundreds of thousands of acres of land just as good as that taken up remain for the homesteaders to file on and when all is under cultivation this section will make for itself a record equal to that of any wheat district in the west. [59]

By November, 1911, Hampton reported 24 houses, a post office, a lumber yard, a store, with a school expected by Christmas. In 1912, School District Number 77 served Hampton

Valley with a "nice school building." Further favorable reports came in from Hampton throughout 1912. "Fall sown rye is two feet high. An orchard with forty trees planted last year is doing well. The gardens are looking fine with radishes, onions and lettuce ready for use." [60]

Rolyat and Stauffer were two nearby desert "communities" which flourished, decayed, died and virtually vanished from the landscape, while Hampton still exists, serving nearby ranches and traffic passing along U.S. 20.

Rolyat

The settlement of Rolyat was located just east of Hampton. The post office Rolyat (Taylor spelled backwards) was established in September, 1910. It was reportedly named for a postal official in Washington, D.C., who had helped the community get its office. In December, 1910, the Rolyat school reported nine pupils. According to reports from Rolyat, the community was a lively one. The ladies of Rolyat formed their own literary club in 1912, a leap year in which they also planned a social to entertain the menfolk. One weekly note from Rolyat read, "The homesteaders are all busy plowing and don't have much time for gossip now, but I guess they will catch up next winter." [61]

One anonymous homesteader did find time to put together his feelings on Rolyat in verse form, when the settlement was indeed part of the "living desert"—

ROLYAT

Say!
Did you ever wish to be,
Some place where the winds are free,
Where "tired feelings" all take flight,
And sweetest dreams are yours by night—
Where sorrows never come, nor pain,
And toil is met in honest gain,
Where there is nothing to combat?
Well, come right out to Rolyat.

Oh, say!
Did you ever look, forsooth,
For the long-lost Fount of Youth,
And give up in mild despair
To a fate of "Peroxide Hair"—
Do you know it really lies
Right here under God's blue skies?
Shall I tell you where it's "at"—
Well right here!
It's Rolyat.

Well, say!
Did you ever want a home—
One to really call your own,
Just a hook to hang your hat?
You've got 'em here
At Rolyat.
R-O-L-Y-A-T
Rolyat as plain's can be!
Hippo! Highpo! one, two, three!
Rolyat's the place for me!

Homesteader [62]

In July, 1912, a letter from Rolyat to the *Bulletin* was included in a special edition of the newspaper. Hope was high that year:

It is surprising to drive through this new country and note the changes and the crops that are growing where there was nothing but sagebrush two years before. I can truthfully say that wheat, rye, oats and barley look as good as in any country I have ever been. We have had more than enough moisture to date to make any of the small grains, and when people speak of this part of Oregon as "High Desert," they are certainly mistaken, and I think they would certainly change their minds if they were to happen through this way. Have plenty of the best fuel, fine water and post timber, and stock can range out all winter. About the only thing we lack is better railroad facilities and we will have them in the next year or two.[63]

The high hopes of the Rolyat homesteaders unfortunately did not materialize, and like neighboring Stauffer to the south and Imperial to the west, the community flourished only a few years before succumbing to the harsh climate.

Stauffer

The High Desert community of Stauffer was located in the Lost Creek Valley, a flat sagebrush plain, elevation about 4200′. Glass Buttes, a 6,385-foot-high bulk of a volcano, is a dominating landmark to the north of the area, while rimrocks hem in the Lost Creek Valley to the west.

Early homesteading in the valley took place between 1910 and 1913. At first, residents wanted to name their post office Lost Creek, but because of duplication, the name Stauffer (after the first postmaster, Charles J. Stauffer) was used. The office opened September 13, 1913. Shortly thereafter, a relative of Stauffer's, Miss Alice Brookings—who was also the teacher of the one-room Stauffer school—took over the mail until 1917, when it was again taken care of at the Stauffer house. Actually, Stauffer was more a collection of scattered homesteads than a town: "There was no general store, no saloon, no public buildings other than the school." [64]

Until they became established and built cabins, most of the homesteaders lived in tents. Lumber was shipped in from Bend or Prineville, or cut from juniper that dots Glass Buttes and nearby rimrocks. Sagebrush, which grows profusely in Lost Creek Valley, was cleared by pulling logs, weighted with rocks, over the sage. This made the brush more flammable, and then the homesteaders would burn it. Supplies including food came from Bend every six months, the journey by wagon taking six days. It was not surprising that a homesteader's grocery list included: "500 lbs of flour, 100 lbs of sugar, 2 sides of bacon, 25 lbs of dried apples, 200 lbs of dried beans." [65]

Fresh vegetables were grown in a small garden near the house and a few cows supplied fresh milk, which was used for making cottage cheese and cheese. Fresh meat was supplied by antelope

The George Young homestead at Stauffer. Contrast the use of juniper for construction with that of lumber-built homestead. Note roll of barbed wire on ground. (Association of Oregon Geographers photo)

Winter homestead scene at Stauffer about 1915. A post office at Stauffer was established in September, 1913. (Association of Oregon Geographers photo)

Homesteader poses in front of his Stauffer cabin. Lumber for construction had to come from mills in Bend or the Maury Mountains. Glass Buttes are in background. Note rifle leaning against cabin, axe on woodpile (Association of Oregon Geographers photo)

Residents of the Lost Creek Valley on a picnic, about 1915. (Association of Oregon Geographers photo)

and deer and the ever-present rabbits and sage hen. Like other desert and grassland communities, rabbit drives were held once a year. Pests other than the rabbit included sage rats and mice; in fact, frequent reports to the *Bulletin* referred to the menace of sage rats. The Glass Buttes area and nearby rimrocks also housed many rattlesnakes.

Lack of reliable water and means to pump water from wells forced the homesteaders to abandon the Lost Creek Valley, only a few years after it had been settled. A 1918 newsletter to Bend stated: "Trouble here at present getting water for our stock as the well which has heretofore furnished an abundance of water is just about dry." [66]

In 1943, the U.S. Army conducted military maneuvers in the Stauffer area, as they did elsewhere in the High Desert. Today, the remnants of some of the homesteaders' cabins are still to be seen among the sagebrush, but apart from stock grazing, Lost Creek Valley is a desolate landscape.

Benjamin Lake

A few miles west of Stauffer, the bleak, dry desert country is interrupted by a number of low depressions in the sand and sage. One of these, Benjamin Lake, is shown on detailed maps of the High Desert. One old map of Oregon, apparently made in a wet cycle, showed Benjamin Lake to be a considerable body of water. It is actually a shallow body of water—small in dry years, large when more precipitation falls.

The lake was approved by both houses of the Oregon State Legislature as a place where "game fish may be propagated and maintained." The measure would have received the Governor's signature had not some people in northern Lake County objected. As soon as ranchers living near Stauffer heard about the proposal to convert the wet-weather lake into a game refuge, action was started to have the measure killed. In reply to efforts to stock a "dry" lake, the ranchers wryly stated:

Most of the stockmen claimed that if the lake was stocked with game fish, the fish would have created a large cloud of

dust and caused much blindness among the sheep and cattle feeding on the green pastures around the lake. It was also asserted that all fish planted in the lake should have been of the dryland variety, and each fish furnished with a large canteen. Alternately, the lake could have been stocked with flying salmon that could return by air every four years to propagate.[67]

The bill, not surprisingly, was vetoed once the facts were known. Today, Benjamin Lake country is the scene of cattle ranching, and at branding time, it has the flavor of the "Old West."

Rabbit drives were common throughout the desert lands of Central Oregon to help reduce crop losses. (Deschutes County Library photo)

A common scene today, similar to above, is cattle raising on the High Desert. Cowboys are seen rounding up cattle on private land or leased public lands abandoned by home-steaders. (Oregon Historical Society photo)

Fort Rock, seen at a distance across a sea of sage and an arid-looking alkali flat.

All the homesteaders needed was power and irrigation water to transform the desert landscape. This Fort Rock Valley scene, taken October, 1976, contrasts with above.

84

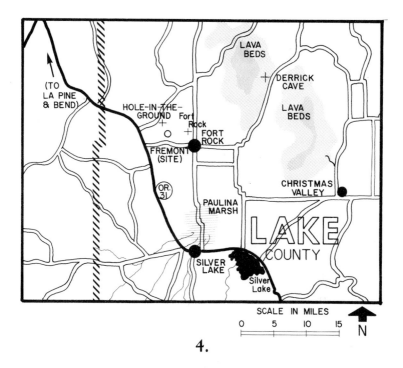

LAVA
BEDS

+ DERRICK
CAVE

LAVA
BEDS

(TO
LA PINE
& BEND)

HOLE-IN-THE-
GROUND   Fort
                    + Rock
     O   + FORT
                   ROCK

FREMONT
(SITE)

OR.
31

PAULINA
MARSH

CHRISTMAS
VALLEY

LAKE
COUNTY

SILVER
LAKE

Silver
Lake

SCALE IN MILES

0   5   10   15   N

4.

FORT ROCK VALLEY

Fort Rock country is perhaps one of the best-known desert areas in Central Oregon. The landmark of Fort Rock, now a state park, has received widespread publicity. Discovery of Indian relics in Fort Rock Cave drew nation-wide attention forty years ago. Of all the desert areas that were homesteaded in Central Oregon, Fort Rock Valley seemed to hold the most promise. However, while a dozen or more homestead communities here have gone beyond the "ghost town" stage, in recent years electricity and irrigation water have helped transform many acres of the inhospitable desert into pleasant, pastoral landscapes.

The historical geography of Fort Rock Valley is interesting. The story begins in Pleistocene times when a vast lake, in places 200 feet deep, occupied much of what is now Fort Rock Valley,

Christmas Lake Valley, Silver Lake and Paulina Marsh (north of the town of Silver Lake).

Early Inhabitants of Fort Rock Valley

At least four shoreline caves within the Fort Rock Lake Basin were the homes of the earliest settlers in Central Oregon—prehistoric hunters about whom Phil Brogan wrote:

Just who these Fort Rock hunters were remains a mystery. Anthropologists who have traced their dim trails through the northern Great Basin can only hazard a guess. Like the "lost men" in the Southwest during Folsom times and the ancient people of the Yuma camps and Sandia caves, the Fort Rock hunters left only their artifacts to record their long stay in this land of vanished lakes. However, it is possible to piece together much about their way of life.

In the Ice Age, or early-recent times, the long fault-block valleys of South-Central Oregon impounded the runoff from a wide region of mountains and basins. This runoff, heavy in pluvial days, formed great land-locked lakes. These lakes, virtually inland seas, reached flood stage and marked their high shore lines through the lashing action of wind-chopped waves. . . . Many small but active volcanoes fringed old Silver Lake, whose waves splashed against the southern slope of Fort Rock Cave. The lashing waters slowly gnawed into the volcanic rocks, creating similar but smaller caves at the bases of various volcanic humps.

As the level of the lake lowered, hunters entered the basin, possibly lured by game that lived close to the shore, where vegetation was dense and prey was plentiful. They likely came from the Great Plains, members of tribes that had crossed the Rockies and moved through the Snake River gateway to the Oregon country.[68]

Indian artifacts, particularly arrowheads, were unearthed in the Fort Rock Valley by homesteaders who occupied the lands shortly after the turn of the present century. In 1928, an ancient Indian burial ground was discovered by Walter J. Perry, a

Deschutes National Forest Service lumberman. The bleached human bones and Indian artifacts—knives, spear points, and arrowheads—were unearthed by winds blowing across the dry bed of the old lake.[69] The following year, the skeleton of an aged Indian woman was discovered in drifting sand close to the Connley Hills (near Fort Rock). The body was partly burned on a funeral pile of sagebrush, indicating that the Indians cremated their dead. The sagebrush, however, did not generate sufficient heat to disintegrate the bones.[70]

In 1930, a forest service crew, engaged in a water development project in the dry Fort Rock country, discovered a spring of bubbling water under drifting sand. Further excavations revealed old arrowheads. Indian tools and weapons, shaped with the fossil bones of animals, were found in October, 1931. One of the tools found was a bone knife believed fashioned from a camel's rib.

In 1938, Dr. L.S. Cressman (University of Oregon professor emeritus of anthropology) methodically excavated through volcanic ash covering the floor of a cave located on the former property of Reub Long, just a short distance from Fort Rock. The excavations led to archaeological finds that attracted nationwide attention of scientists and prompted further detailed search for clues as to how the first inhabitants of the Fort Rock Valley had lived.

The greater "find" in the cavern pumice was some 70 sandals or moccasins, woven by the aborigines from bark of sagebrush (still the dominating vegetation of the valley). About 6,600 years ago, a tremendous explosion in the southern Cascades sent clouds of billowing volcanic ash over vast areas of Central and Eastern Oregon and into Washington and southern Canada. Mt. Mazama (the remnants of which now hold Crater Lake) blasted forth cubic miles of ash which—helped by strong westerly winds—showered the Fort Rock Basin with drifting pumice. Rangeland used by deer and antelope was smothered with volcanic ash, which also filled openings of caves used by the Indians.

Because the sandals that were unearthed in the initial excavation by Dr. Cressman had been treated with a preservative, they could not be used for radio-carbon dating. Further excavation in the same cave by D.B. McFadyn led to the discovery of more sandals, and these had not been treated with preservative, at least not until one of them was made available for Geiger counter studies. Age of an object through use of an "atomic calendar" ascertains how recent the object is, in a radioactive sense. Testing established an age of 9,000 years but later research in the area indicated that Indian families had been hunting in the Fort Rock Valley as long ago as 13,000 years—several thousand years before Egyptians had simple villages and practiced agriculture.

The cave—long known as Cow Cave—is not a very conspicuous part of the Fort Rock landscape. From a distance, it is discernible only as a dark hole set against a cliff. Close up, it is little different from other caves, being about 35 feet wide at the opening and no more than 25 feet deep. The lava roof slopes to the rear of the cave. Large rocks, darkened by smoke, overhang the entrance. One unique feature of the cave, however, is the entrance, sloped and smoothed by the action of the waves that were whipped up by winds blowing across the huge lake that flooded the Fort Rock basin in a more humid period.

The cave provided refuge for livestock seeking shelter from winter storms sweeping down from nearby Mt. Newberry. Little of archaeological interest is to be seen now as excavations have been completed, the pumice in the cavern restored and smoothed, and weeds and sagebrush grow over piles of screening in front of the shelter. In June, 1963, it became officially Fort Rock Cave and was registered as a national historic landmark. This was made possible by the late Reub E. Long and Mrs. Long who, at that time, owned the land where the cave is located.

People are still lured to Fort Rock Valley to hunt arrowheads and other Indian artifacts. Those who know the likely places and have the patience to sift desert sands return repeatedly to enjoy their hobby. As stated earlier, when Fort Rock Valley was first settled in the landrush days early in this century, home-steaders found on the shores of the old lake scores of arrow-heads, javelin points and spearheads. One early rancher, the late George Menkenmaier, whose lands were later held by Reub Long, collected an estimated 10,000 in the Fort Rock Basin. When word got out that Fort Rock Cave had been occupied thousands of years ago by Paleo-Indians, interest in collecting artifacts greatly increased. The basin has now been extensively searched and good finds are rare.

Fort Rock

The prominent landmark, Fort Rock, was discovered in 1873 when the unusual formation attracted the attention of a William Sullivan who was seeking stray cattle in the area. The rock's physical features and the origin of the name were described in 1905 in *An Illustrated History of Central Oregon*:

Fort Rock, one of the most peculiar rock formations to be found in the west, is situated just sixteen miles north of Silver Lake. It is so named because it is a natural rock-walled fort, enclosing about thirty-five acres of land, with a rock wall averaging 300 feet high. The fort is circular in form and rises from a level plain many miles from the surrounding mountains. The wall is about 200 feet thick at the base and thirty-five feet wide at the top. Outside it rises perpendicularly, but there are several places on the inside where by exercising care and caution one may scale it. Such a feat is impossible from the out-side. At the south side of the fort there is an opening less than one-eighth of a mile wide which makes it easy of access.

There is no particular legend or tradition among the Indians regarding Fort Rock. They say it has always existed so far as they know. It was never used as a fort or place of refuge during tribal wars. The name Fort Rock was given to the formation by the early settlers owing to its resemblance to a fort. During the warm, sultry days of summer, cattle and horses in the neigh-borhood seek the sheltering shade of the high rock wall. The only use ever made of Fort Rock was occasionally as a round-up corral by cattle and horsemen. During the years to come, thousands of people will visit this curiosity from all parts of the country, and possibly in the future Silver Lake will be one of the noted places on some trunk line railroad, where tourists will be advised to stop and see the sights.[71]

No trunk railroad came to Silver Lake but the "natural curiosity" mentioned above has been sustained. Dr. Bruce O. Nolf, professor of geology at Central Oregon Community College, commented as follows on Fort Rock:

Fort Rock is the eroded C-shaped remnant of a tuff ring, a type of maar volcano built by repeated "base surges" of ash directed radially outward at high velocity from a central vent. The central vent of Fort Rock volcano is now covered by material washed from the slopes, and the southwest wall of the ring has been breached by the erosion of waves on ancient Fort Rock Lake. The eruptions forming tuff rings occur when rising basaltic magma encounters abundant ground water at significant depths beneath the earth's surface, causing a violent steam explosion which drives a highly compressed column of fragmented ash, steam, and water rapidly upward to the surface. At the ground surface the base of the eruptive column expands at high velocity, depositing wet ash in a ring-like form which is concentric about the vent.

Other, more deeply eroded remnants of tuff rings dotted the Fort Rock basin, including the low north rim of the tuff ring in which the famous sandal cave occurs, west of Fort Rock. Hole-in-the-Ground, approximately six miles west of Fort Rock (and described below), was formed by a similar, but shallower, steam explosion, which deroofed the explosion chamber very violently.

Base surge eruptions build tuff rings in many other parts of the world, including Diamond Head, in Hawaii, and modern base surge eruptions are well known in the Philippines, Azores, and Galapagos.

Conspicuous and impressive from a distance, Fort Rock also deserves close-up inspection. Its volcanic mass takes on changing appearances when viewed from different nearby positions. Then the cliffs, grey from a distance, take on a variety of micro-

View across Fort Rock Valley from Cow Cave, where Indian artifacts were excavated in 1938 by Dr. L.S. Cressman.

"C-shaped" remnant of volcanic Fort Rock. Walls rise 300 feet from desert lake basin. Fort Rock is now a state park. (Oregon State Highway photo)

Unusual vista from the rim of Fort Rock looking across desert and remnants of more volcanic tuff rings. (Oregon State Highway photo)

Wave-cut terrace on flanks of Fort Rock. Waves from vast lake once lapped against and eroded volcanic remnant.

colors—bright yellow, whitish yellow, orange—where lichens cling to the weathered rocks. Its perpendicular walls seem impenetrable and inhospitable to all but birds that make their homes in the pitted cliffs. Some of the major species of nesting birds here include the prairie falcon, red-tailed hawk, grey-horned owl, white-throated swift and several species of swallows.

Only from nearby can you see that storm-tossed waves eroded the cliffs of Fort Rock. The wave-cut terraces—curved and amazingly smoothed in a desert landscape where angular shapes usually are more representative of arid landforms—are best seen from just inside the crescent of Fort Rock. A bumpy dirt road circles the inside walls of the tuff ring. From this road, fairly easy access can be gained to the roof of the promontory where widespread vistas reward the climber.

The landscape spread out at the foot of Fort Rock is uninterrupted in all directions. The green bulk of Mt. Newberry dominates the skyline to the northwest. Elsewhere, the more distant skyline—a succession of blue hills, mountains and mesas —frequently does not stand out in the hazy, dusty atmosphere of the Fort Rock basin. Close inspection of the southern fringes of the valley reveals a series of steep-sided fault scarps. The basin floor, a flat plain, unbelievably flat at 4,400 feet elevation, is largely an indescribable grey color. In marked contrast to the general sand and sagebrush landscape, there is a checkerboard of green acres irrigated by the hidden waters. These are the waters that teased and eluded the early homesteaders and defied man until electricity and pumps were introduced to the Fort Rock Valley.

As is true with other desert areas in Central Oregon and elsewhere, wind plays an important role. At Fort Rock, winds swirl around the rocks in gusts, seemingly coming from one direction, then another. Out across the valley floor, dustdevils skip across green fields, then resume their whirling journeys through sage and sand. Except for Fort Rock Village—which when viewed from atop the rock seems like a collection of buildings huddled together for company in the lonely plain—there are few signs of habitation. This is ironical when we find that, in 1909, the *Bulletin* reported, "hundreds of newly built homes and tents may be seen from the summit of Fort Rock prominence."[72] Today, when man has far more control over his environment, only a scattering of homes, some mobile, are to be seen.

Although Fort Rock has been designated as an Oregon State Park, and electric stoves, picnic tables and restrooms have been provided, the landscape today is still largely a physical one. A small enclosed cemetery adjacent to the park area seems to accentuate the supremacy of nature. Walk through this rather barren cemetery. Note the ages of the dead and the recorded years of death and the first flush of homesteading days is recalled.

Homesteading Fort Rock Valley

Early in the twentieth century, homesteaders—not water—flooded the Fort Rock Valley, perhaps enticed by the Homestead Act, or perhaps attracted by the appearance of the natural landscape at that time. A government publication, *Climatology of the United States* (1906), stated that the Fort Rock Valley had from ten to twenty inches of precipitation and that "crops can be grown in nine-tenths of these states (Washington and Oregon) without irrigation." Reub Long, in discussing the impact that man and animals have made on the natural environment in the Fort Rock country, stated:

I have lived in the Fort Rock-Silver Lake area since 1900. When my father came to Lake County, about 100 years ago, the country was covered by bunch grass. Deer were scarce, and in most places there was very little browse. There were few livestock until the Indians were put on reservations after the Bannock-Paiute War in 1878.

From 1880 settlement was rapid. The range was used hard by thousands of semi-wild horses; by homesteaders' livestock; by thousands and thousands of sheep owned by itinerants; by sheep and cattle by hundreds of legitimate livestock operators of Nevada, California and Oregon. From 1880 to 1900 was the

Fort Rock became the background setting for an episode of the film "Way West" in the mid 1960's. Most of the movie was shot on location in Central Oregon, including desert scenes on the sand dunes near Christmas Valley. (Bend Chamber of Commerce photo)

Early-day homestead south of Fort Rock. Cow Cave is located 300 yards west of this ranch, which is still in operation. (Josephine Godon photo)

heyday of the bonanza livestock operators, typified in Oregon by Pete French, John Devine, and Bill Brown. Nevada had dozens of such men whose herds of horses, cattle and sheep ran to 50,000 head each or even up to 100,000. Many of these grazed in Lake County part of the time.

By 1900 livestock herds began to dwindle due to crippling losses in dry years or hard winters; lack of feed; dry cycles; activities of homesteaders; and the advent of barbed wire. Many, many who had been millionaires for a time, went broke. All over the area one could see ex-millionaires tending bar, acting as janitors, or working as buckaroos for forty dollars a month.

At the same time the range vegetation changed completely. Sagebrush, always present but kept in check by the better adapted grass, began to "assume dominance," as the scientists expressed it. Rabbitbrush, also present everywhere, came into the abandoned fields of homesteaders and occupied areas after fires had swept through. Deer numbers began to increase, encouraged by more browse, more water supplies, fewer domestic livestock.

In 1909 a new homestead act was passed, allowing a man 320 acres of non-irrigable land, and in 1916 this was increased to 640 acres. The result was a rash of homesteaders from 1909 to 1920. This affected the desert forage, too. They all had horses and they plowed up millions of acres that should have been unplowed. Forage declined, causing further decrease in domestic livestock, and greater amounts of sage and rabbitbrush.[73]

However, one geographer, James Buckles, doubted that bunch grass was ever dominant in the valley and that "homesteaders destroyed the sagebrush by burning, plowing and overgrazing, at the same time creating a myth that the Fort Rock Valley had been a valued winter range because of the great amount of bunch grass that grew there." [74]

Misleading information in railroad publications may well have attracted many homesteaders. A prospectus on Lake County, found in an abandoned homestead in the Fort Rock Valley, stated, "The soil consists of a rich black loam and grows wheat, which will average 60 bushels to the acre. All varieties of fruit

Reub Long Ranch on the edge of the Fort Rock Desert. Note non-native trees established on ranch, and power lines strung across hills in the background.

Wire fence separates contiguous properties, in Fort Rock Valley. The property on the right of the fence shows overgrazing and wind erosion. That on the left shows bunch grasses and soil stability.

such as apples, pears, prunes, plums, cherries, and all other kinds of berries grow in abundance." [75] Such advertising of climate, fertile soils, agricultural opportunities and land available for homesteading were lures which brought homesteaders to the area. The settlement of the Fort Rock Valley took place rapidly:

Homesteaders flocked in all over the desert from 1905 to about 1915—a few after that. Little towns began to spring up everywhere. Within a couple of looks, we had such promising new "towns" as Fremont, Lake, Sink, Fleetwood, Connley, Arrow, Buffalo, View Point, Cliff and Loma Vista. [76]

Most of these towns, however, were nothing more than a post office-store, serving homesteaders who settled in the vicinity.

This sudden transformation of the desert was recorded by cartographers who, hitherto at a loss for what to mark on maps of the Fort Rock Valley, were suddenly besieged with the listing of new settlements. At its peak, the Fort Rock Valley had a population estimated to have been between 1000 and 1200 persons. [77]

Weekly reports from Fort Rock to Bend were encouraging, like those from the Millican and Hampton Valleys. For example, a 1909 communication to the Bend paper from S.M. Findley, a farmer in the new Fort Rock settlement, stated:

A large number of homeseekers are taking up land in this locality and hundreds of newly built homes and tents may be seen from the summit of Fort Rock prominence, from which the surrounding level and fertile plateau takes its name. To the south and east of the rock, the houses and tents and newly plowed fields dot the land as far as the eye can see. Mr. Findley says that he recently refused $4000 for his 160-acre tract, nearly all of which he has under cultivation. It is generally believed that the Fort Rock country will, in time, be one of the greatest wheat-producing sections in the state and the fact that excellent water for domestic purposes is easily accessible by means of wells, is resulting in the land being rapidly taken by homesteaders. [78]

Two scenes of a Fort Rock Valley homestead. Close study of lower photo reveals variety of utensils used by homestead family. (Josephine Godon photo)

99

The fertility of the Fort Rock Valley was attributed to the formation of soil by stream deposition. The bunch grasses and tall sagebrush were regarded as further evidence of this fertility. Not surprisingly, the area was thought to be ideal for stock raising or for growing grains, especially wheat. Indeed, in the fall of 1912, nearly 10,000 bushels of grain were threshed in the Fort Rock Valley. Five schools operated in the area, plenty of wood for fuel and fence posts was available from the nearby forest reserves, and a sawmill nearby furnished lumber for homes.

The community of Fort Rock was started in 1908 in the midst of what was described as attractive country. In an interview with an old-timer in 1940, the *Oregon Journal* reported: "When I came in March, 1910, I never saw a more beautiful country. It was covered with bunch grass. Cattle were fat. Grass and crops were good and the people content." [80]

Goods were freighted in to Roy Nash's store and post office from the nearest railhead, which at that time was at Shaniko. Fort Rock grew with the building of a hotel, a creamery, another store, three feed barns, a blacksmith's shop and several houses. The town boasted a newspaper, the *Fort Rock Times*, which was published every Thursday, starting May 23, 1913.

Small-town newspapers usually provide an insight into community life. The weekly *Fort Rock Times* was no exception. Local gossip, news of trips taken and visitors to town made page one, but other news and advertisements helped piece together the picture of the social and economic life in the area. Not surprisingly, farming successes and problems were of major concern:

August 6, 1914:
The song of the mower is heard in the land. People are busy securing their rye where the rabbits have been considerate enough to leave anything to harvest.

August 26, 1915:

With the mercury soaring up in the nineties and frequent dust storms, life in the sagebrush has not been all poetry the past two weeks.

August 6, 1914:

H.F. Swingle finished cutting his rye this week, getting about 20 tons from 50 acres which is to be considered good after the way the frost nipped it.

Fremont was one of the larger homestead settlements in the valley. It was started in 1908 by I.R. Fox from southern California and by other homesteaders from Portland and the Willamette Valley. By 1912, it was reported to be one of the "most industrious settlements in Central Oregon." It boasted a store, a post office, and a schoolhouse that was a "credit to any new settlement." Further, there was a regular Sunday school. On alternate Saturdays the library literary society gathered. It was said that, in the immediate vicinity of Fremont, rye, turnips, rutabagas and wheat were growing well in the decomposed volcanic soil, which was from three to five feet deep and easily worked.

The outlook for dairying in the Fremont country was, at that time (mid-1912), reported to be good, and a creamery and cheese factory had been started. Late in 1912, the factory was turning out "lots of number one cheese" six days a week. However, the advent of drought, which was later largely responsible for the abandonment of the desert lands, was noted by 1915, only a few years after homesteading in the desert had started. It was reported that water holes that had never been reported short of water before were so dry that there was insufficient water for range livestock and barely enough for personal use.

Social events periodically involved visits and picnics to ice caves such as Derrick Caves, which had recently been discovered. Fourth of July celebrations in Fort Rock seemed well-planned, patriotic events. The *Fort Rock Times* issue of June 22, 1916, called for residents of the valley to spend the Fourth in town to watch or to participate in horse racing (1st prize, $5.00), foot

Fremont country, in Fort Rock Valley, seemed like fertile land to homesteaders in 1914. Rye grown here was an important source of feed for livestock. (USFS photo)

Fremont, at the height of the homesteading about 1915. (Josephine Godon photo)

racing (1st prize for 100 yards, $1.00), children's races, and a literary program with songs and speeches. The evening was capped off with a fireworks display and a dance featuring a twenty-piece brass band from Silver Lake.

Subscribers to the Fort Rock newspaper were asked to bank at LaPine or Bend, to use the Lakeview Title Company, or seek dental, physician or notary needs in Fort Rock. The Fort Rock Hotel provided "good clean beds, best home cooking and a feed barn." Those out-of-town subscribers were attracted to the area by the following advertisement, August 6, 1914:

Do you want a homestead? If so, northern Lake County should be your destination. The Oregon Eastern Railroad will run through this territory. 320 acres may be had with lots of pasture land in the foothills. For information, write to the U.S. Land Office, Lakeview, Oregon.

Isolated as the Fort Rock Valley was, government red tape in handling necessary supplies sometimes compounded the problem. In 1914, a shipment of 1200 pounds of seed rye was to have been shipped by parcel post from Burns to Fort Rock, 120 miles away. Instead of going to Fort Rock by pack horse or other conveyance, it had to follow the prescribed mail route. The seed was hauled to Prairie City, then shipped over the Sumpter Valley Railway to Baker City, then taken to Portland, 350 miles away. From there, the seed was shipped to Sacramento, California, to Reno, Nevada, and on to Lakeview. From Lakeview it was loaded on a star route stage and hauled to Fort Rock.[81] Though several railroad surveys were made, all that materialized from them were false hopes and some settlement for land speculation, such as the town of Ficksburg, which was platted in the center of the Fort Rock Valley in anticipation of the railroad.

The successes in the Fort Rock Valley were hard to come by. Edwin A. Eskelin, son of a Finnish-born homesteader who moved from Michigan to Silver Lake in 1909, described homestead life early in the twentieth century:

During the early homestead days, even those acquainted with agriculture did not pay any attention to the fact that the market was far away and the roads were poor. Each farm was more or less self sufficient and the people being satisfied with such as they had. The roads were where the people started to travel, and if one set of ruts became too deep, they would drive beside the deep ruts, or if (in the timber) the storms blocked a road, the people would drive around the blockade. They would cope with the dust in summer, and snow and mud in winter.

For enjoyment, parties and dances would be held, dancing to such music as was available. Newspapers and magazines were available in almost any language so the whole family could read in the evenings. Under those circumstances, illiteracy was unknown, even with the limited school education. The parents of children made every effort, even under difficult circumstances, to provide their children with at least some formal education.[82]

Formal schooling took place in one-room schools in which the turnover of teachers was remarkably high. Eskelin also described how his father fashioned a plow from a square sheet of metal and juniper timber; and he recalled harvest time, when the first crop of hay (rye) was gathered. For several years, life in the Fort Rock Valley revolved around such agricultural activities.

The climate of Fort Rock country became increasingly arid around 1917-1918; precipitation for 1917 was only 4.45 inches. Silver Lake had dried up in 1889, and ranchers from many parts of the Fort Rock Valley farmed small acreages in the lake bottom. Elsewhere, well water was fast lowering and crop failures became common. In addition, the growing season in the valley had always been extremely short, except for 1906 when, at Silver Lake, 137 frost-free days were recorded. Still, the average length of the frost-free season at Silver Lake (for the period 1896-1924) was 74 days; during six of these years the period was shorter than 50 days.   Very few plants are able to survive and mature in such a climate.[83]

During 1918 and 1919, reports from the Fort Rock area were mostly bleak. Water became a major problem. The drought had a dramatic impact on the Fort Rock Valley, as dry farming became more and more precarious. Evidence of the rapid population

Eskelin Ranch, Fort Rock Valley. Mature trees shelter ranch house from wind, and shade it from summer sun. Barn and windmill, left, go back to the homestead era.

Electricity and water are key factors in the changing landscape of Fort Rock Valley. Behind the substation are plowed fields and alfalfa. In foreground, desert land awaits reclamation.

decline is shown by the closing dates for various post offices including: Arrow, February 28, 1918; Cliff, June, 1920; Connley, July 31, 1920; Fremont, May 15, 1919; Loma Vista, May 31, 1918; Sink, August, 1920; Woodrow, May 15, 1916.

Some believed that water lay beneath the surface and this led to some optimism:

> Despite the fact that there has been somewhat of an exodus from the Fort Rock Valley during the past three years, there is no cause, according to F.C. Eckelmeyer, a large land holder in that part of Lake County, for farmers of that big valley to lose hope. The homesteaders in this section are poor and need funds to carry on this work or need for someone to provide capital investment for the farmers. A geological expert is needed to study water possibilities.[84]

In 1919, an irrigation district was formed. This was regarded as the last chance to save valley agriculture. Seventy-five homesteaders had been starved out. In October, 1921, a test well was sunk at Fort Rock by State of Oregon geologists, as an eager crowd of 100 anxiously stood by:

> A mother's remark to her small son—too young to take any interest in mere water—revealed perhaps more clearly the feelings of these people and the new hope which the success of the test well had brought into being. "Look at all that water; isn't it pretty," she said happily to the youngster at her side. It was only water, somewhat muddy at that but to her and to the many gathered about the spot it meant everything.[85]

Dry farming became a losing fight for most ranchers. The water brought to the surface was slightly alkaline—causing concern that irrigation would leave deposits of salt on the soil and prove a further hindrance to farming. Late in 1921, there was talk of a pipeline to tap Paulina Lake for gravity flow to provide water for livestock grazing on 253,000 acres of bunch grass. But homesteaders were moving out and, by 1924, only a trickle of homesteaders were arriving in the area. Further trouble occurred in

The Bend-Silver Lake mail stage (1917) makes its way through forests and snow. (USFS photo)

The community of Silver Lake serves nearby ranchers and motorists traveling Highway 31 between La Pine and Lakeview.

Picture Pass and block-faulted ridge southeast of the town of Silver Lake. In the foreground, wheel ruts of pioneer wagons skirt the sandy edge of the old bed of Silver Lake. (Kathy Bowman photo)

Grave marker (right) commemorates the tragic loss of life in the Christmas Eve fire at a community hall at Silver Lake in 1894.

1925 when flames destroyed half the town of Fort Rock—the general store, a residence, and two small vacant buildings. Reub Long had this to say about homesteaders in the Fort Rock area:

> The homesteaders were beaten one by one. Those who arrived with the least stayed the longest. The ones who came with money usually came without experience and hired the others. The result was that the well-to-do who came with money and no experience left with experience and no money. . . .

> So the homesteaders left, their cabins and houses were mostly taken or burned and nothing is there now but some rusting barbed wire, a few juniper posts and maybe a broken dish and a busted wagon wheel.[86]

The Town of Silver Lake

A prominent American geographer, Isaiah Bowman, described the town of Silver Lake in Fort Rock Valley in 1930:

> Settlement ventured far in the High Desert between Bend and Burns but still farther in the Low Desert that includes Fort Rock Valley and Christmas Lake Valley. There are about twenty-five houses between Silver Lake and Fort Rock. Not a single one is inhabited. If the house is not boarded up, the windows have all been broken or the place is in ruins. The sheds have not been in use for a long time. The yards are unkempt. Sagebrush is all about. A third of the houses in the town of Silver Lake are unoccupied and the windows broken. There are no sidewalks. Heavy dust lies everywhere. Sage grows right up to the back yards.

> The town boasts a good high school and grade school with five teachers and about eighty pupils. Some of the parents move into the village when winter sets in and stay until spring. When the town was first built, supplies were brought in and produce shipped out a month's journey to The Dalles on the Columbia. When the railroad reached Shaniko in 1900 the haul to rails was cut in half. Things were then thought better; and they were thought excellent when rails reached Bend, 70 miles away in an airline. The roads are unimproved prairie tracks, but the big highways creep nearer.

Everyone talks about the present "dry cycle," the rain famine of the last two years. Those that are left tell of discouraged neighbors who have moved away. At least the snows of winter are as light as the rains, and that pleases the sheep herders; but the dry-farming crops need a moist ground, and it is winter snow and rain that supply it. Every dry-land farmer, whether in Oregon or Montana, wants plenty of snow. Though the sage country looks hopeless, the ground water is so near the surface that it can be recovered easily; and at one point there is irrigation from shallow wells served by diesel engines.

Between Fort Rock and the eastern border of the Deschutes National Forest, in a distance of ten miles, there are 15 uninhabited and 2 inhabited houses on or quite near the road that runs through the driest and worst part of the valley. There are perhaps twice that number of houses on the hilly border of the plain, but they were too far away for me to see (August, 1930) whether they were occupied or empty. In the midst of the plain lies Fremont, once an occupied hamlet and now wholly abandoned. Fort Rock has but two or three occupied houses besides the combined post office and general store. In all of the ranch yards there are windmills if the house is occupied, and half of those unoccupied have this lingering sign of the hopeful homesteader.[87]

The population of the Fort Rock Valley declined from 1000 in 1915 to about 100 in 1941.[88] Late in the 1930's, the U.S. government took about one quarter of the land in the area out of private ownership and put it under government supervision. Not until the 1950's was power brought to the Fort Rock country and Silver Lake. The proposal to extend the Rural Electrification Authority line from LaPine to northern Lake County was made in 1953. Two years later, amid considerable celebrations at Silver Lake, the long-awaited power arrived.

In anticipation of the October 28, 1955, power arrival, the Bend newspaper, on October 13, carried an editorial which summarized the history of Silver Lake and recognized the significance of electricity for the community:

There was a time, in the long ago, when Silver Lake, close to the northern rim of the Great Basin in Oregon, was an important town on the dusty road of pioneer days that reached from the Columbia to Lakeview. But over a period of some four decades the historic town, stopping place of freighters and rangemen in pioneer days and shopping center for a region larger than some eastern states, suffered a decline.

In 1920, the town had a population of 126, as the homesteading era passed. The 1930 census listed a population of 122, and in 1940 there were only 87 people in the community. Shortly after that date Silver Lake gave up its status as an incorporated city. As a result there was no population listing in 1950.

Now Silver Lake faces a comeback. Apparently it will be the metropolis of the interlocked basins to be reclaimed through the use of electricity for pumping purposes. Nearby Fort Rock will serve the reclaimed area as an important community center. Power lines in the region will not be energized until October 28, when a celebration will be held in Silver Lake, but already the pioneer town is showing new life. New business firms are being established, new houses are going up, a gain in school attendance has been noted.

Silver Lake is expected to assume its role as an important interior Oregon town without any fuss, for it already has experienced the problems of a city. And behind Silver Lake is a history more venerable than that of some of its neighbors, including Bend. The Silver Lake post office was first established in 1875—over 80 years ago. The first post offices were at farm homes, but it was not long until the town of Silver Lake came into existence, to serve a rangeland empire. Then in the homesteading era in the late nineties and in the early years of the present century, Silver Lake became a bustling town, with a population greater than that of Bend or Redmond in the same period. Its old rival, in the region north of Lakeview, was pioneer Prineville.

The history of the early-day town was that of a typical rangeland village, where freighters and cowmen, "drummers" and sheepmen intermingled. A part of Silver Lake's pioneer history was tragic. On December 24, 1894, a fire swept through a building in which a Christmas eve party was being held, in an upper floor hall. Forty-three persons died in that fire. It was the greatest loss of life suffered in a single tragedy in the history of Oregon.

On Friday, October 28, when power and light came to the tri-basin region of Fort Rock, Silver Lake and Christmas Lake— Silver Lake will be host to all Oregon. The occasion will mark Silver Lake's debut as an important city in the region first explored by the Pathfinder John C. Fremont.[89]

Kathy Bowman gives us a look at Silver Lake as it is today, close to half a century after Isaiah Bowman's description in this section:

"We've had our best luck lookin' fer water around the edge of the basin. . . ."

". . .and they had two and a ha'f rows plowed under b'fore they realized they had that second crop comin' up underneath!"

Snatches of shop talk like this issue from the counter in the little plywood-construction cafe as several men of the Silver Lake basin take a leisurely late-morning coffee break on a dry, winter-sunshiny day. Sitting casually on the red plastic seats of the chrome-plated barstools, they sip their hot black coffee and make observations to each other in the easy dialect of Silver Lake residents. Occasionally the waitress, taciturn with strangers, exchanges a smile and a pleasantry with one of the burly, winter-bundled men. The men wear nearly identical work-worn leather boots with traces of dry-basin silt still clinging to the sturdy uppers. They discuss the two things that affect the welfare of almost everyone in the Silver Lake region —well water and alfalfa hay. Now and then a sage observation floats through the warm cafe air—"A fellow has to be a damned optimist to make a livin' this way."

The community of Silver Lake is a hodgepodge of old and new. Cozy, dark older houses, aluminum-shiny trailers and starkly new-looking highway businesses make up the bulk of this tiny town.

There is a reserved dignity about the people and the buildings here, reflecting the solemnity of the surrounding desert. Even the trailer houses sit farther apart than necessary, for somehow the openness and privacy offered by the desert become an ingrained necessity.

The older homes are fenced and comfortable in the wide-open setting. By contrast, the brilliantly white walls of the gas station, the newly painted cafe and the little grocery store have not yet been assimilated by gradual weathering into the look of the desert. Still, they serve the needs of ranchers, loggers, travelers and the Forest Service employees from the government quarters across the ridge, who are all part of the sparse network of humanity that laces across the landscape.

From the narrow constriction of Picture Pass—an opening in the block-faulted ridges south of Silver Lake—the view of the valley is reminiscent of some giant kindergartener's simple puzzle left stretched out on the huge floor. Large pieces of subtly varying scenery—ditch-lined fields, pastures, odd remnants of volcanic mountains—make up most of this big puzzleboard. So suddenly was the game abandoned that one piece of the whole was left tilted on edge, forming a long, gracefully sloping triangular ridge which turns the blue of jewels as the winter sun descends on the far side of the steep slopes.

Through the low pass, the asphalt highway winds down among the coarse rocks, crossing and recrossing a crude, worn trail in the lava left by the wheels of many wagons. Later the new road parallels the old one along the shores of pasture-like Silver Lake. This time the old roadway is not a rough and rocky surface. Instead, the perfect pair of firm wheel ruts wander along the sandy edge of the old lake bed.[90]

Pioneer things tend to resist time better than things today. This old road is no exception, for it withstands even the fierce, scouring winds of this country amazingly well. Today these ruts stand six to eight inches above the loose sand that once was the level of the roadbed, sculptured by the whipping winds.

Along the roadside as you drive back to the little town from the south is one of the oldest features of the community, as well as one of the most prominent. Level and brushless, the lake bottom land was cleared in the early 1900's for a pioneer cemetery. Still in use today, the small graveyard is dominated by a single twelve-foot monument inscribed with dozens of names and ages—toddlers, adults, and children, of different families but all together.

Why did all these people die at once? Local inquiry revealed that this large, hulking monument, rimmed by a low cement curb, honors the memory of pioneer people who perished in a community hall fire during a celebration many years ago.

The rest of the graves here are mostly well tended, for this cemetery is still in use. New, shiny brown granite stones and recently laid gravel occasionally join the delicately engraved intricacies of fine-grained old white marble, heavy, primitive-looking stones of dark rock and the fading inscriptions of wooden tablets, all marking graves of old timers. Like any pioneer graveyard, families are mostly buried together—grandparents, mothers, fathers, children, the sons- and daughters-in-law and their children—all lie in one area. Here they are honored together, often with loving inscriptions wrought by the then-important stone carver's art.

At the opposite end of town, the smooth asphalt road passes on its fill bed through a gently twisted marsh of shallow streams and shrubby trees. Suddenly in the sunlight, two winter-bared white fans of quaking aspen trunks are split by the road, creating a natural port-of-entry on this side of town. In summer this collection of straight, white, black-flecked trees with rigid white branches is softened by the smooth contours of many rustling, bright yellow-green heart-shaped leaves.

The vehicles that run between these trees and on into the desert reflect the people who use them. Husky, healthy, desert-weathered individuals with traces of valley silt still clinging about them, both men and machines of the Silver Lake basin are shaped by the desert environment.[90]

Hole-in-the-Ground

As mentioned earlier, Hole-in-the-Ground is a maar volcano six miles west of Fort Rock. Approaches are usually from Fremont Highway to the west or from Fort Rock to the east. Either way, a drivable dusty dirt road brings visitors to the edge of the mile-wide crater. Here the open desert of the land slopes upward to meet an attractive pine and juniper forest. The transition from the desert to the forest is abrupt, showing best on an aerial photo.

The setting of Hole-in-the-Ground reflects interesting studies on the effects of microclimate—the climate of a small, distinct

Hole-in-the-Ground from the south rim. Large rocks in the foreground were ejected by the explosion which created the crater.

Isolated Fort Rock appears like a submarine sailing across a barren plain, as seen from the outer rim of Hole-in-the-Ground. Note abrupt transition from forest to desert.

area. While most of the south-facing slope of the inside of the crater is largely sagebrush and grass and the crater floor is a mixture of sagebrush and pumice, ponderosa pine dot the sun-sheltered northern rim.

The crater is remarkably circular in shape, but the eastern rim is perceptibly higher than the western rim. Rocks of various sizes thrown out by the explosion testify to the force (estimated by Peterson and Groh to be equal to five million tons of TNT [91]). The rim around Hole-in-the-Ground offers visitors extensive views of the snow-capped peaks of Bachelor Butte and South Sister to the northwest and of the forested slopes of the Paulinas to the north. From the eastern side of the rim, the visitor over-looks the desert lands of Fort Rock Valley.

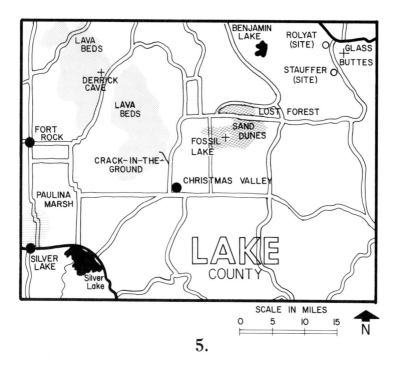

5.

CHRISTMAS LAKE VALLEY

Christmas Lake Valley is an eastward continuation of Fort Rock Valley with similar landscape. Sagebrush and open sandy areas extend for mile after mile in all directions. From ground level, except for the prominent rimrocks and fault scarps to the south, and volcanic craters to the north, only giant steel power lines and abandoned homesteads rise above the flat plain. Each contributes to the feeling of isolation of the area. The power lines indicate that somewhere to the south, at the receiving end of the line, there are humming industries, bright neon signs, and cities bustling with human activity. The desert of Central Oregon appears only as some geographical space that must be bridged to carry electricity south from the Columbia River.

The homestead cabins, small dilapidated shacks scattered throughout the plains east of Christmas Valley, are almost obscured by the tall sagebrush. These cabins are little different from those found elsewhere in the desert lands of Central Oregon. But Christmas Valley—origin of the name is unclear—is now taking in "new homesteaders," and another type of "land rush" has developed. In 1961, a California firm purchased 70,000 acres, or 108 square miles, of sagebrush-studded real estate in Christmas Valley from a cattle company for $10 an acre. The cattle company had previously purchased most of the land from Lake County at 25 cents an acre. Lake County had acquired much of the land through possession following delinquent taxes.

The development of the property was, in part, geared to creating a rural retirement area with part-time farming to add to pension income. Plans called for the creation of an artificial lake, a golf course, air strip, motel and a water system. An intensive advertising blitz in urban areas of California followed—and worked. By mid-1966, 99 percent of the development was sold and several thousand people had purchased land in Christmas Valley, reportedly paying as high as $1100 an acre. However, by the end of the year, only 50 to 60 families had settled there, not enough to support the commercial businesses that had been established.

Most of the parcels of land sold ranged from 20 to 40 acres, in country that takes 60 acres of improved Christmas Valley land to graze one cow for a year.

"Disappointments over the quality of the land purchased were common, and twenty-five percent of those who purchased land asked for and received their money back after viewing their property. Others defaulted on their payment contracts." [92] Several "For Sale" signs, many weathered and faded, are still to be seen on the sandy surface of the land adjacent to the highway leading into Christmas Valley from the west. Yet, most of those who have settled there are enthusiastic. They say that the wide-open spaces, the clear skies, fresh air and recreation opportunities in the area are major assets.

Christmas Valley is a community literally set down in a sea of sagebrush. From a distance, the low profile of the town barely

The isolated community of Christmas Valley barely shows in the vast sagebrush plains, once the bottom of a large interior lake in Central Oregon.

This photo, taken from the same rimrock as above, shows the impact of water on the desert landscape.

119

Left: Cracked alkaline soil, tall sagebrush, and forlorn-looking homestead cabins combine to create a pathetic landscape scene east of Christmas Valley. Right: Two abandoned windmills have not drawn water for years. Their crumbling structures still rise above the alkaline soil and sagebrush north of Christmas Valley.

A brewing summer thunderstorm adds gloom to this abandoned homestead in the Christmas Valley plain.

rises above the sage on the flat plain. In town, mobile homes and conventional houses are scattered around the "downtown" center—a surprising array of commercial activity for such a small, isolated town. Two motels, attractive and clean, are set back from the main highway from Silver Lake to Christmas Valley, on the edge of town. A trailer park, almost filled with trailers and campers, is adjacent to one motel.

The town boasts a general store, a tavern, two gas stations, an air strip and rodeo grounds. However, the focal point for most activities is the Christmas Valley Lodge which has restaurant facilities and a cocktail lounge, but is not designed to accommodate guests. The lodge is an imposing structure, somewhat out of place when compared to the glitter of nearby aluminum mobile homes. The dominant architectural features of the lodge include the large, glassed A-frame center which anchors ranch-style construction on each end. A large lava-rock fireplace chimney towers over the split shake roof. Inside the lodge, diners are able to look across a compact 9-hole golf course flanked on one side by a 30-acre man-made lake. This lake— the home of numerous wild fowl—and the summer green of the golf course contribute to the almost bizarre cultural landscape of Christmas Valley, virtually an oasis in a desert landscape of sand and sage.

Beyond the golf course to the north, desert lands rise. Sagebrush gives way to juniper where topography influences greater precipitation. Beyond the junipers, the skyline is dominated by a volcanic landscape of black lava and the youthful appearance of cinder cones—the Four Craters Country, depicted in the aerial photograph.

Christmas Valley Lodge is the focal point for different groups of people. Some come to explore for fossils and Indian artifacts in the Christmas Valley area; others to ride dirt bikes over the nearby sand dunes. All inevitably start the day with breakfast at the lodge's restaurant and finish the day with dinner there. The lodge caters to golfers, to realtors who wish to talk "land" in the less business-like atmosphere of the restaurant, and to local residents who drop by for conversation and coffee. Cowboys from nearby and distant ranches converge on the lodge in the evening, especially on Saturday evening, when the in-style of clothing is definitely western.

Once the sun has set, the dry desert air rapidly disperses the warmth accumulated during the day. At night the desert skies literally glisten with stars, and the morning air is bright and clean. Distant hills and rimrocks on the horizon stand out in such clarity that they seem but a few miles from town. Morning chill (on an October visit the minimum temperature was about 10 degrees F!) quickly melts under the desert sun and is replaced by a warm and comfortable atmosphere conducive to outdoor physical activity.

Christmas Valley is well situated for the exploration of areas of both historical and geological interest, especially Crack-in-the-Ground, Fossil Lake and the Lost Forest.

Crack-in-the-Ground

A unique geological feature located eight miles north of Christmas Valley is a two-mile-long crack or fissure in the earth's surface:

Open cracks or fissures in the earth's surface are not uncommon; they occur fairly often as a result of earthquakes or volcanic activity, but they usually become filled with rock rubble or lava and disappear in a very short time. A large fissure that stays open for hundreds of years is, therefore, a rare feature. Such a fissure occurs about eight miles north of Christmas Valley. It is a deep, narrow rift about two miles long and it has remained open for perhaps a thousand years. For lack of any official name, the fissure is referred to simply as "Crack-in-the-Ground."

Crack-in-the-Ground is closely related to the Four Craters lava field on Green Mountain, one of the many isolated centers of recent volcanic activity within the high lava plains of Central Oregon.

The Four Craters lava field was formed from basaltic lava that flowed mainly south and east from craters along a fissure.

Acres of sagebrush and sand: The paved highway from Silver Lake to Christmas Valley passes many similar scenes. Few acres have been developed, except in the town of Christmas Valley.

Christmas Valley Lodge, the focal point for visitors and residents of the area. The Lodge has dining room and cocktail lounge. Two adjacent motels offer accommodations.

123

Left: Aerial view of Crack-in-the-Ground and Four Craters Volcanoes and lava flow. Right: Close-up of one of the Four Craters. (USFS photos)

The awesome-looking chasm of Crack-in-the-Ground slices through the Oregon desert north of Christmas Valley.

Sluggish flows piled up a layer of black spiny lava on the slightly sloping Green Mountain lava surface. Four cinder cones aligned along the fissure rise from 250 to 400 feet above the lava surface. The distance from the northernmost cone to the southernmost is roughly two and a quarter miles. The freshness of the lava and lack of soil and vegetation on the surface indicate a recent age for the field.

Crack-in-the-Ground is a tension fracture in basalt. The walls are rough and irregular and show no lateral, and but very slightly vertical movement. Although the crack is open for a distance of more than two miles, it then continues to the northwest and southeast as a trace, which although not visible on the ground, is revealed on aerial photographs. Where best developed, the fissure is from ten to fifteen feet wide at the top, narrowing downward. The depth varies, but is as much as seventy feet in some places.

Crack-in-the-Ground opened before the last volcanic activity, and at its northwest end a tongue of lava piled up, tumbled into, filled and buried the chasm for several hundred yards. The opening of the fissure probably took place no more than 1,000 years ago. Erosion and weathering have been at a minimum, but over the many years the Crack-in-the-Ground existed, some rock has sloughed off the walls, and sand has blown or washed in to fill the bottom. At several places the walls have slumped, thus bridging the gap and allowing access to the deeper parts of the fissure. Winter ice is sometimes preserved during the summer in the deeper, more cavernous places where cold air is trapped.

Crack-in-the-Ground is a relatively fresh geologic feature. This stark freshness is partly the result of subdued chemical weathering in arid climate and a lack of any recent violent earth movements or renewed volcanic activity in the immediate area.[93]

The giant fissure was known to homesteaders in the Christmas Valley area and was the scene of many picnics. Ice found in caves in the crack was used for making ice cream.

In places it is possible to walk along the chasm floor, with entrance easily obtained where a dirt road bisects the fault. The floor of the fissure is rocky in parts and sand-covered and flat in other places. The almost vertical walls of basalt tower skyward up to 70 feet, shutting out direct sunlight.

A dirt road from Christmas Valley Lodge heads north for three miles, then east one mile, creating an avenue through the tall, grey sagebrush. Though the road is in good driving condition, the powdery alkaline soil resting on the roadbed is easily disturbed by autos. Clouds of white, choking dust smother everything that dares disturb it and sends telltale signals as to where any vehicle is moving over the valley roads.

The last three miles of the road to Crack-in-the-Ground are over a rather rough road, as it climbs out of the valley floor through a lava- and juniper-studded landscape. From any one of a number of prominent points on the lava ridges, extensive views to the east include glimpses of the valley below with occasional views of white alkaline lake beds—remnants from the time when both Fort Rock and Christmas Lake Valley were large, shallow lakes.

Fossil Lake

For many people, the thought of sand dunes in Oregon (except along the coast) may be hard to imagine. How can this, the beaver state, land of webfoots, notorious for incessant rain (except for the 1976-1977 winter!), lush grass, and green landscapes be also the home of sand dunes? Yet, desert sand dunes, 12,000 acres of them, are located about twenty miles northeast of the community of Christmas Valley. They are known to few tourists and even rarely visited by Central Oregonians. Hollywood, though, has not ignored the dunes; a movie set was located there for the filming of a portion of "The Way West" in the late 1960's. One of the earliest accounts of the sand dunes dates back to travels E.D. Cope (a noted paleontologist) undertook in 1877. This description of the dunes and of the desolation of the surrounding area is still as valid today as it was a hundred years ago:

One day we made an exploration of the desert in the direction of Wagontire Mountain towards the north-east. After

View from juniper-studded lava ridge across Christmas Lake Valley. White alkaline flats are vivid contrast to sagebrush plain.

Aerial view of sand dunes. Ribbed appearance is due to seasonal shift in wind. (USFS photo)

traversing the sagebrush for two hours we reached the sandy desert of which we had heard. An apparently endless expanse of sand dunes extended to the west, the north and the east. These dunes were not conical, but had a sloping side to the south-west, and a perpendicular face to the north-east. As the wind blew strongly from the south-west, the sand slowly crept towards the summit, and then fell in a fine shower to the base below. In this way the dunes constantly shift their position north-eastward till they reach the slopes of a range of hills, where they are banked up so as to be visible at a long distance.

The sand I found to be soft and difficult for man and beast. At intervals there are shallow ravines lined with bunches of coarse grasses. At one of them I found a set of Indian domestic implements; a flat dish and several pestles carved so as to have a portion for the hand separated from the head by a shoulder. All were made of the vesicular basalt, and some of them were colored red, like that found on the slopes of Winter Mountain. As no camp could well have continued there, it appeared that these implements had been left or thrown away. This sandy desert is said to be about twenty-five miles from east to west, and half as wide from north to south.

We left the sand and kept the sage-brush until about twenty-four miles east of our camp. Here I climbed a cliff to view the country. It was composed of the same thinly stratified volcanic mud-conglomerate as the hills that bound Silver Lake on the north. Lizards of the genera Uta and Sceloporus abounded.

The scene was impressive from its wild desolation. As far as the eye could reach was the same sage-brush desert, the same waterless region of death. Many a man has entered this region never to escape from its fatal drought, especially during the first days of the overland emigration to Oregon.

The Wagontire mountain, whose long and gloomy mass made the northeastern horizon, owes its name to the disastrous fate of one of those trains of emigrants. Coming from the east, they reached the mountain with parched mouths and eyes aching from the heat and dust, expecting to find water for themselves and animals. . . .[Finding no water] the horses gave out in endeavoring to continue their way through its fastnesses. They lay down and died, and nothing remained of the party but a few whitened bones, and the iron tires of the wagon wheels.

Towering sand dunes create a realistic desert landscape near Fossil Lake. The dunes provide playgrounds for bikes and dune buggies.

Wagontire Mountain, elevation 6,504 feet, is seen here from U.S. Highway 395 near Wagontire, Oregon. The mountain, which lies in both Harney and Lake counties, was so named because an old wagon tire lay beside the road on its northern slope for many years. This tire was said to have come from an emigrant wagon which was burned by Indians. (Oregon State Highway photo)

Many experienced hunters have been lost in this desert, and two years after my visit, one of the oldest rangers of Oregon entered it, and was never heard of afterwards. And it is indeed easy to miss the few small springs that are found at remote intervals in this desolation of one hundred and fifty miles diameter east and west and north and south.

We mounted our horses, and were glad to retrace our steps before darkness should overtake us. We kept along the southern boundary of the sand dunes as a guide, and at last struck our outward-bound trail. To reach our camp was then not difficult, and we were soon busy housekeeping round the campfire. After a night's refreshing sleep we returned by the way we came, to Silver Lake. [94]

Despite the fascination of the sand dunes, most of the scientific interest in this part of the Christmas Valley centers on adjacent Fossil Lake. In 1876, Oregon Governor John Whiteaker, while camping in Central Oregon in the neighborhood of Silver Lake, noticed some fossil bones on the surface of the open prairie. Convinced that he had discovered an important fossil bed, he brought it to the attention of Professor Thomas Condon of the University of Oregon. Condon went to Fossil Lake in 1876, and wrote of his visit:

Considering the narrow area of this fossil bed, a surprisingly large number and variety of fossils were found and so brought to the light of scientific report. The last part of the journey took us through a monotonous dead level covered with sagebrush, until finally we reached the home of a ranchman on the shore of one of those strange inflorescences of alkali. Here we left our wagon and the next morning started on horseback for the fossil beds. After traveling about eight miles, we saw, from the eminence of a sand dune, an apparent circular depression four or five miles across, in the lowest portion of which was a small pond, or lake, surrounded by grass and *tule* bushes.

Perhaps two miles to the leeward, this depression was bordered by a line of sand dunes, unquestionably formed from sands blown from the bed of the lake that once occupied the whole of this depression. It is the blowing out of this sediment which exposes the fossils buried in the depths of the old lake. Here we staked our horses and went to work. We found many fragments of elephant bones, a fine collection of bird bones, the bones of a large horse, a large camel and the remains of a smaller animal of the camel family, the Auchenia, which Professor Cope named in honor of Governor Whiteaker, Auchenia Vitakeri.

Judging from the uniformity of its surroundings, one is found unavoidably thinking of an extensive lake sediment, of which this fossil lake is only a very small portion. The original lake probably included Silver Lake and Klamath Marsh with its surroundings, and perhaps Summer Lake and an extension eastward over the present Harney and Malheur Lake regions. These waters were lowered to their present level by evaporation in excess of inflow. The mineral left behind accumulated in the process until it covered the face of the pond like snow.

These waters must have varied in extent at different periods. From one spot, the writer could mark an extent of not less than sixty miles from east to west and fifteen to twenty from north to south, with a variation of surface scarcely reaching what an ordinary eye would call thirty feet. And this whole extent was water-covered during the life of the elephant, as is proved by his remains. The portions of this extensive lake bed, which remain latest, caught most of the animal bones buried in its mud. This special one we visited continued sandy and when dry, its contents were laid bare by drifting winds.

The fossils of these Silver Lake beds were found often lying on the surface, bare of any covering. The sands and dust that had covered them were blown to the leeward where they now lay in extended dunes; and this uncovering and drifting process was still visibly going on. Among these fossils we found many arrow heads of obsidian, such as were used by recent Indians. We found, too, lying among them, many fresh-water shells of species now living in the waters of Klamath Marsh. Shells and arrow heads were, like the fossil bones, entirely uncovered, lying upon the surface of the ground.

If the sands, the fossils, the arrow points and the fresh water shells were all of the same period, and the fossil bones were early Pleistocene, then the arrow points were fashioned before the glacial age and men inhabited the surrounding hills in the early Pleistocene period. But the mixture of these facts may be due entirely to the simple law of gravitation, for both the arrow points and the recent shells may have settled down among the fossils as the dust and sand upon which they rested were gradually blown away.

The rarest and most valuable fossils collected on this expedition were the eighty bird bones which were unusually perfect and in a fine state of preservation. Later they were sent to an Eastern scientist for classification and never found their way home. Fortunately they had been examined by an expert in the study of fossil birds and to him we are indebted for much interesting knowledge of the life of the region. Dr. Schufeldt tells us that here at Fossil Lake lived five species of gulls, two of terns, eleven species of ducks, four of geese, one of which "must have been nearly as large again as our common wild Canada goose." There was also a large species of swan named for Governor Whiteaker, Vitikeri. There were great horned owls, blackbirds, coots, herons, crows, eagles, grouse, prairie hens and a great cormorant. "But the strangest figure upon the scene among the birds was a true flamingo."

And found with these bird bones, Dr. Shufeldt also enumerates the fossil mammals as including a great sloth as large as a grizzly bear called the Mylodon, and at least four kinds of camels, ranging in size from a modern camel to the smaller llama. There were also bears, coyotes, rabbits, gophers, otters, beavers, a mammoth elephant and three species of the modern type of horse or Equus. These "Equus Beds" are considered among the richest yet discovered of the early Pleistocene period. It is interesting to note the variety and great abundance of the fossil remains of the camel and the horse whose families are represented among the oldest fossil mammals of the Northwest. And here we find both lines persisting with unabated vigor even to the beginning of the glacial ice.[95]

Professor Condon reported the findings at Fossil Lake to Dr. E.D. Cope, noted vertebrate paleontologist of Philadelphia. Cope visited Central Oregon in 1879, and was followed by a succession of visits from noted scientists from that time. Dr. Cope wrote of his visit and his discoveries:

We left the lake by the low pass on the northeast, and, passing by the flat that held Thorne's Lake when it existed, drove to Christmas Lake, our first stopping-place. This is a small body of water of but few square miles in extent, and is excessively alkaline. Its waters have no appreciable effect on the arid shores, which were dry and dotted with the sage brush almost to its edge. I found abundance of larvae of dipterous insects, and crustaceans, as Cyclops, in the water; but a rancher who lived near by, told me that it contained no fishes, a statement which I could readily believe. Avosets (Recurvirostra) and stilts (Himantopus), waded in the shallows, feeding, I suppose, on the invertebrate life which I observed. From the rancher I obtained some beautiful obsidian arrow-heads and scrapers which he found at Fossil Lake.

By early the next evening we had reached the "bone yard." We dug two holes in a low place, one for ourselves and one for the horses, getting clear water, somewhat alkaline to the taste, at a depth of about eighteen inches. We soon had a brisk fire of dry sage brush; and bacon and mutton, potatoes and canned tomatoes, were soon in condition to satisfy the appetite which only the camper in the dry regions of the West experiences. We rolled up in our blankets, and my last thoughts before entering dreamland were of what I should find on the morrow.

The "bone yard" was found by cattlemen who were looking up stock which had wandered into this forbidden region, and many of the best specimens were carried off by them and lost to science. The first naturalist who visited it was Professor Thomas Condon, of the University of Oregon, at Eugene, who, with the care for scientific research which has always distinguished him, saved many good specimens and brought them home to his museum. One of these was part of the jaws of the remarkable llama, of about the size of a mule.

Subsequently my assistant, Mr. Charles H. Sternberg, of Lawrence, Kansas, visited the place, and made what is probably the largest collection ever made there.

There were two species of true horses (Equus) both extinct; and a huge sloth (*Mylodon sodalis*, Cope) as large as a grizzly

bear. The mammoth (*Elephas primigenius* Blum.) was represented, together with numerous smaller mammals of species
both recent and extinct. There were coyotes, otters, beavers,
gophers (Thomomys), moles and rabbits, and the phalange of a
bear; but no peccaries, tapirs, raccoons or opossums, which one
would find in similar company in corresponding beds in the
eastern states.

Then there were multitudes of bones of birds and of fishes.
These were all of existing genera and often species. I detected
a few novelties, as a swan (*Cygnus palorcgonus*); a goose,
(*Anser hypsibatus*), and a cormorant, (*Phalacrocorox
macropus*). One of the most abundant species was a grebe,
which I could not distinguish from the one so commonly seen in
Silver Lake, (*Podiceps occidentalis* Lawr). Other species still
await determination. Of the fishes, all belonged to the families
of chubs and suckers, and several of them to species still living
in the Silver and Klamath Lakes.

The next day I set out early to explore the ground. I found it
to be a slight depression, embracing perhaps twenty acres,
which was devoid of sage brush, but was dotted with occasional
plants of greasewood (*Sacrobatis vermicularis*), a fact due to
the presence of water beneath the surface. The latter was,
however, perfectly dry, and consisted of a light-colored mixture
of sand and clay, or a dried lacustrine mud of volcanic origin. It
was perfectly movable by the wind, and of indefinite depth.

Fragments of bones and teeth were not rare. The most
abundant were those of the large horse, *Equus occidentalis*
Leidy, and the *Holomeniscus licsternus* Leidy. I also found bones
and fragments of the *Elephas primigenius*, and the greater part
of the skeleton of a Thomomys. I obtained, in fact, repre-
sentatives of most of the species previously discovered, including numerous birds and fishes. All were on or in the loose,
friable deposit. Portions of the surface were white with the
shells of the *Pianorbis* (*Carinifex*) *newberryi* Lea, a species
which is still living in Klamath Lake.

Scattered everywhere in the deposit were the obsidian implements of human manufacture. Some of these were of in-
ferior, others of superior workmanship, and many of them were
covered with a patine of no great thickness, which completely

Fossil Lake elephant leg bone. Both femur and tibia were broken. Only one toe bone was missing. (Dr. Ira S. Allison photo)

Residual lake materials stand like small islands where wind has removed surrounding lake bottom. Searching for fossils on lake bed still proves lucrative.

replaced the natural lustre of the surface. Other specimens were as bright as when first made.

The abundance of these flints was remarkable, and suggested that they had been shot at the game, both winged and otherwise, that had in former times frequented the lake. Their general absence from the soil of the surrounding region added strength to this supposition. Of course it was impossible to prove the contemporaneity of the flints with animals with whose bones they were mingled, under the circumstances of the mobility of the stratum in which they all occurred. But had they been other than human flints, no question as to their contemporaneity would have arisen.[96]

Further discoveries at Fossil Lake have been made over the years and numerous scientific reports are to be found in various journals on natural history. One of the most interesting discoveries was the remains of a sea-going salmon, for it indicated that the interior of Central Oregon, at some time in the distant past, had a water link with the Pacific Ocean. When the lake over-flow stopped, the salmon became land-locked, but salmon and other fishes lived at Fossil Lake until aridity took over. Many of the vertebrate species are now extinct.

During the colder and wetter climate of the Pleistocene, about 10,000 to 12,000 years ago, the Fort Rock-Christmas Lake basin was flooded by waters of melting glaciers. Fossil Lake, now but a tiny wet-weather pond or playa in a down-faulted lowland, is measured in feet, but it was once part of a body of water extending 40 miles across. As with Fort Rock, previously described, wave-cut cliffs and beaches represent the fluctuating marks of former shore lines where nomadic tribes established campsites in their quest for game. Over a period of several hundred thousand years, Fort Rock Lake fluctuated widely in levels as climatic changes occurred.

Indian artifacts are still found throughout the fringes of the Fort Rock and Christmas Lake valleys. These archaeological finds help piece together the story of early man's existence in Central Oregon. As the climate of the area became increasingly arid, over a period of many years, the large lake shrank

Crescent-shaped dunes encroach on Lost Forest east of Fossil Lake. (USFS photo)

Ponderosa pines growing out of sand-covered hills in the Lost Forest east of Christmas Valley.

Wind-blown sand begins to hide man's attempt to divide and demark land ownership.

138

dramatically in size. Deflation by wind—starting about 4,500 to 7,000 years ago—scoured the dried lake sediments from the basin floor and started piling dunes on the lee side of the valley. This process continues today. Indeed, it is advisable not to visit Fossil Lake and the sand-dunes area on extremely windy days. It can be a gritty experience, and the danger of being stuck in drifting sand is a real one.

Fossil Lake is perhaps the largest deflated basin, extending several miles across. To the east are the depositional features of the desert landscape, dunes as high as 40 feet and about 1000 feet or more in diameter. The surfaces of the dunes are ribbed in a complex pattern because of seasonal shifting of the prevailing winds. Scientific studies of the composition of the dunes reveal that the sand grains are a mixture of volcanic and sedimentary derivation, with the larger percentage being volcanic pumice and ash, deposited as a result of the Mount Mazama (Crater Lake) explosion, some 6,600 years ago.

Resistant layers of rock in the area have been left isolated as wind has carried away the more friable material. Fossilized bones, shells and teeth, including large bones from elephants and horses, have been picked up out of the surface sand or by digging into loose sand.[97] Many of the Fossil Lake mammal bones, estimated at about 70,000 years old, are displayed at the American Museum of Natural History or at the Museum of Paleontology of the University of California at Berkeley. It is probably true to say that Fossil Lake, Oregon, is far better known to out-of-state scientists than to many Oregonians.

Fossil hunting continues today, with amateurs having the greatest success after windstorms have swept more loose sand from the lake basin. However, it is interesting to note that relatively few people in Central Oregon are acquainted with Fossil Lake, an area studied scientifically a quarter of a century before Bend became a town.

The Lost Forest

The Fossil Lake sand dunes are drifting eastward and have encroached on a 9000-acre stand of ponderosa pine. What is unique about this desert landscape is that this "Lost Forest" is about forty miles from any main stands of ponderosa pine, and continues to survive the arid climate of the region.

Approaching the area from the north (on the Frederick Butte road which originates on Highway 20 east of Brothers), one is amazed by the sudden transition from sagebrush to forest. For no apparent reason, along an almost straight line, the sage stops and the pines, mixed with junipers, begin. However, these pines are not as tall as ponderosas usually are, and are more widely spaced. The topography within the forest is undulating, with buttes and ridges throughout the area.

Ponderosa pine normally grows where precipitation averages about 18 to 30 inches, much above the 8 inches experienced in the desert lands of northern Lake County. Geologists, foresters and tourists have long been bewildered by the Lost Forest, probably the remnant of an extensive pine forest that once covered much of Central Oregon. As the climate over Central Oregon became more arid, the large forest diminished and the desert landscape took over—except for the Lost Forest.

Scientific studies of the forest were conducted in the 1950's after logging had removed over-mature and insect-affected trees. Foresters from the BLM and the U.S. Forest Service dug down to the roots of a ponderosa pine and discovered that below the sand there was a hard chalk-like substance which undoubtedly was the bed of an ancient lake which once covered the area. For a few inches above this hardpan the large, shallow roots of the pine were contained in moist sand. These large roots had an unusual number of hair roots to lift moisture from damp sand. It was reasoned that the 8 inches of annual precipitation had no runoff, a minimum of evaporation, and was held by hardpan until used by the pines and juniper roots.

Surveying notes in 1877 described the area as being quite heavily timbered with strong indications of water near the surface. An abundance of bunch grasses everywhere was reported but, today, there is little evidence of these grasses.

With a notable absence of young trees and the prevalence of diseases and insects, the Lost Forest is gradually vanishing.

Furthermore, there is evidence that precipitation has decreased during this century, accounting in part for the lack of young trees less than 50 years old.

Reports from a retired forest ranger who knew the area 50 years ago indicate that at one time several springs ran all summer. Today there are no known springs though Mounds Spring—located west of Lost Forest—suddenly became active after 35 years. During the homestead era it was an excellent watering place but disappeared in the dry years that followed. Arrowheads found in the vicinity indicate that Mounds Spring served as an Indian campsite.

As the migrating sand dunes push relentlessly eastward through the area and aridity continues, it is likely that the Lost Forest will, in time, be replaced by a desert landscape.

NOTES

1. Ada Hastings Hedges, *Desert Poems* (1930), p.4.
2. *Oregon: End of the Trail*. Oregon Writers' Program, W.P.A. (1940), p. 464.
3. *An Illustrated History of Central Oregon* (1905), p. 739.
4. Preston James, *Geography of Man* (1959), p. 47.
5. Israel Russell, *Geology and Mineral Resources of Central Oregon* (1905).
6. See 1889 map facing page 1.
7. Agnes Campbell, *Fragrance of Sage* (1939), p. 85.
8. Kathy Bowman, unpublished manuscripts, 1976.
9. Ellis Lucia, *Klondike Kate* (1962), p. 134.
10. *Bulletin*, Feb. 1, 1960.
11. Urling Coe, *Frontier Doctor* (1939), p. 34.
12. Agnes Campbell, *Fragrance of Sage* (1939), p. 85.
13. Ronald Taylor and Rolf Valum, *Wildflowers 2. Sagebrush Country* (1974), p. 17.
14. Ibid.
15. *Bulletin*, Sept. 28, 1905.
16. *Ibid.*, Dec. 29, 1909.
17. *Ibid.*, Apr. 13, 1910.
18. Ronald Taylor and Rolf Valum, *Wildflowers 2. Sagebrush Country* (1974), p. 12.
19. George Palmer Putnam, *In the Oregon Country* (1915), p. 67.
20. Ada Hastings Hedges, *Desert Poems* (1930), p. 53.
21. Urling Coe, *Frontier Doctor* (1939), p. 227.
22. *Bulletin*, June 16, 1953.
23. Ellis Lucia, *Klondike Kate* (1962), pp. 130-131.
24. Agnes Campbell, *Fragrance of Sage* (1939), pp. 162-163.
25. *Bulletin*, Jan. 25, 1911.
26. *Ibid.*
27. Agnes Campbell, *Fragrance of Sage* (1939), p. 32.
28. *Ibid.*, pp. 33-34.
29. H.L. Davis, *Honey in the Horn* (1935), pp. 364-366.
30. *Bulletin*, Apr. 15, 1914.
31. *Ibid.*, Aug. 25, 1909.
32. Ada Hastings Hedges, *Desert Poems* (1930), p. 58.
33. Isaiah Bowman, *The Pioneer Fringe* (1931), pp. 94-95.
34. *Ibid.*, pp. 97-99.
35. Urling Coe, *Frontier Doctor* (1939), pp. 228-237.
36. Kathy Bowman, unpublished manuscript, 1976.
37. Dallas Lore Sharp, *Where Rolls the Oregon* (1914), pp. 49-54.
38. *Bulletin*, Nov. 29, 1916.
39. Israel Russell, *Geology and Mineral Resources of Central Oregon* (1905), p. 76.
40. *Bulletin*, Nov. 16, 1927.
41. *Ibid.*, Aug. 16, 1907.
42. *Ibid.*, July 3, 1912.
43. *Ibid.*, Oct. 19, 1910.
44. *Ibid.*, July 3, 1912.
45. *Ibid.*, Apr. 30, 1913.
46. *Ibid.*, Apr. 16, 1913.
47. Israel Russell, *Geology and Mineral Resources of Central Oregon* (1905), pp. 76-77.

48. Lewis L. McArthur, *Oregon Geographic Names* (1974), p. 87.
49. Kathy Bowman, unpublished manuscript, 1976.
50. Norman Peterson, Edward Groh, Edward Taylor, Donald Stensland, *Geology and Mineral Resources of Deschutes County, Oregon* (1976), p. 34.
51. *Bulletin*, Apr. 2, 1937.
52. *Ibid.*, July 8, 1914.
53. *Ibid.*, Mar. 1, 1911.
54. W.A. Rockie, *Northwest Science* (1944), p. 36.
55. *Bulletin*, Mar. 16, 1918.
56. Israel Russell, *Geology and Mineral Resources of Central Oregon* (1905), p. 25.
57. *Ibid.*, p. 65.
58. *Bulletin*, Feb. 10, 1934.
59. *Ibid.*, Apr. 20, 1910.
60. *Ibid.*, June 19, 1912.
61. *Ibid.*, Oct. 16, 1912.
62. *Ibid.*, Apr. 24, 1912.
63. *Ibid.*, July 10, 1912.
64. Don Van Home, *Oregon Geographer* (Fall, 1976), p. 3.
65. *Ibid.*, p. 10.
66. *Bulletin*, June 12, 1918.
67. *Ibid.*, June, 1928.
68. Phil F. Brogan, *East of the Cascades* (1964), pp. 21-22.
69. *Bulletin*, June 2, 1928.
70. *Ibid.*, Nov. 4, 1929.
71. *An Illustrated History of Central Oregon* (1905), p. 868.
72. *Bulletin*, Apr. 14, 1909.
73. *Ibid.*, Mar. 20, 1963.
74. James Buckles, "The Historical Geography of the Fort Rock Valley, 1900-1941," MA Thesis, University of Oregon (1959), p. 52.
75. *Ibid.*, p. 58.
76. E.R. Jackman and R.A. Long, *The Oregon Desert* (1964), p. 34.
77. James Buckles, p. 52. (See #74)
78. *Bulletin*, Apr, 14, 1909.
79. *Ibid.*, July 3, 1912.
80. *Oregon Journal*, Jan. 28, 1940.
81. *Bulletin*, May 20, 1914.
82. Edwin Eskelin, *History of the Eskelin Family* (unpublished) 1974.
83. James Buckles, p. 31. (See #74)
84. *Bulletin*, July 12, 1919.
85. *Ibid.*, Oct. 3, 1921.
86. E.R. Jackman and R.A. Long, *The Oregon Desert* (1964), pp. 41 and 55.
87. Isaiah Bowman, *The Pioneer Fringe* (1931), p. 186.
88. James Buckles, p. 31. (See #74)
89. *Bulletin*, Oct. 13, 1955.
90. Kathy Bowman, unpublished manuscript, 1977.
91. Norman Peterson and Edward Groh, *The Ore Bin* (Oct. 1961).
92. *Bulletin*, Aug. 4, 1966.
93. Norman Peterson and Edward Groh, *The Ore Bin* (Sept. 1964).
94. E.D. Cope, *The American Naturalist* (1889), pp. 981-982.
95. Thomas Condon, *Oregon Geology* (1910), pp. 121-125.
96. E.D. Cope, *The American Naturalist* (1889), pp. 977-979.
97. Ira Allison, *Fossil Lake, Oregon* (1966).

BIBLIOGRAPHY

Allison, Ira S. *Fossil Lake, Oregon*. Corvallis: Oregon State University Press, 1966.

Appleton, Jay. *The Experience of Landscape*. London: John Wiley and Sons, 1975.

Baldwin, Ewart M. *Geology of Oregon*. Ann Arbor, Michigan: Edwards Bros., 1964.

Bedwell, Stephen F. *Fort Rock Basin—Prehistory and Environment*. Eugene: University of Oregon, 1973.

Bowman, Isaiah. *The Pioneer Fringe*. New York: The American Geographical Society, 1931.

Brodatz, Phil and Dori Watson. *The Elements of Landscape*. New York: Reinhold Book Corp., 1968.

Brogan, Phil F. *East of the Cascades*. Portland: Binford & Mort, Publishers, 1964.

Buckles, James S. "The Historical Geography of the Fort Rock Valley, 1900-1941." MA Thesis, University of Oregon, 1959.

Bulletin (Bend), 1903-1976.

Campbell, Agnes. *Fragrance of Sage*. London: John Long, Ltd., 1930.

Clark, Keith and Lowell Tiller. *Terrible Trail: The Meek Cutoff*, 1845. Caldwell, Idaho: The Caxton Printers, Ltd., 1967.

Coe, Urling C. *Frontier Doctor*. New York: The Macmillan Co., 1939.

Condon, Thomas. *Oregon Geology*. Portland, Oregon: The J.K. Gill Co., 1910.

Conron, John. *The American Landscape*. London, Toronto, New York: Oxford University Press, 1973.

Cope, E.D. "The Silver Lake of Oregon and Its Region." *The American Naturalist*. November, 1889.

Courtney, Dale E. "The Oregon Desert, 1967: A Pioneer Fringe?" *Yearbook of the Association of Pacific Coast Geographers*. Vol. 29, 1967. Corvallis: Oregon State University, 1967.

Cressman, L.S. *Petroglyphs of Oregon*. Eugene: University of Oregon, 1937.

Davis, H.L. *Honey in the Horn*. New York, London: Harper and Brothers, 1935.

DeVoto, Bernard. "The West: A Plundered Province." *Harper's Monthly Magazine*. August, 1934.

Eskelin, Edwin A. "History of the Eskelin Family." (not published) 1974.

Fort Rock Times. Fort Rock (various dates).

Friedman, Ralph. *Oregon for the Curious*. Portland, Oregon: Pars Publishing Co., 1965.

Harper, Frank B. "Dust to Dust." *Oregon Journal*. January 28, 1940.

Hatton, Raymond. *Bend Country Weather and Climate*. Redmond: Mid-State Printing, 1973.

Hedges, Ada Hastings. *Desert Poems*. Portland, Oregon: Metropolitan Press, 1930.

Hill, Beth and Ray. *Indian Petroglyphs*. Seattle, Washington: University of Washington Press, 1974.

Hine, Robert V. *The American West: An Interpretive History*. Boston: Little, Brown, & Co., 1973.

Illustrated History of Central Oregon. Spokane: Western Historical Publishing Co., 1905.

Jackman, E.R. and R.A. Long. *The Oregon Desert*. Caldwell, Idaho: The Caxton Printers, Ltd., 1964.

Jackson, Donald D. *Sagebrush Country*. New York: Time Life Books, 1975.

Jaeger, Edmond C. *The North American Deserts*. Stanford, California: Stanford University Press, 1957.

James, Preston B. *A Geography of Man*. Boston: Ginn & Co., 1959.

Kirk, Ruth. *Desert, The American Southwest*. Boston: Houghton Mifflin Co., 1973.

Krutch, Joseph W. *The Voice of the Desert*. New York: William Sloan Associates, 1967.

Larson, Peggy. *Deserts of America*. Englewood Cliffs, N.J.: Prentice-Hall, Inc., 1970.

Lucia, Ellis. *Klondike Kate*. New York: Ballantine Books, 1962.

McArthur, Lewis L. *Oregon Geographic Names*, Portland, Oregon: Oregon Historical Society, 1974.

McCornack, Ellen C. *Thomas Condon, Pioneer Geologist of Oregon*. Eugene: University Press, 1928.

Peterson, Norman V. and Edward A. Groh. "Crack-in-the-Ground, Lake County, Oregon." *The Ore Bin*. Vol. 26, No. 9. September, 1964.

Peterson, Norman V. and Edward A. Groh. "Hole-in-the-Ground" *The Ore Bin*. Vol. 23, No. 10. October, 1961.

Peterson, Norman V., Edward A. Groh, Edward M. Taylor, Donald E. Stensland. *Geology and Mineral Resources of Deschutes County Oregon*. Portland: State of Oregon Department of Geology and Mineral Resources, 1976.

Pratt, Alice Day. *A Homesteader's Portfolio*. New York: The Macmillan Co., 1922.

Prichard, Walter H. *Chewaucan*. New York: Vantage Press, 1967.

Putnam, George Palmer. *In The Oregon Country*. New York, London: G.P. Putnam's Sons, The Knickerbocker Press, 1915.

Rockie, W.A. "Backsight and Foresight on Land Use." *Northwest Science*. Vol. XVIII, No. 2. May, 1944.

Russell, Israel. *Geology and Water Resources of Central Oregon*. Washington: Government Printing Office, 1905.

Sharp, Dallas Lore. *Where Rolls the Oregon*. Boston and New York: Houghton Mifflin Co., 1914.

Shufeldt, R.E. "Review of the Fossil, Fauna of the Desert Region of Oregon." *Bulletin American Museum of Natural History*. Vol. XXXII, 1913.

Taylor, Ronald J. and Rolf W. Valum. *Wildflowers 2. Sagebrush Country*. Beaverton, Oregon: The Touchstone Press, 1974.

Van Home, Don. "Stauffer." *Oregon Geographer*. Association of Oregon Geographers. Vol. 10, No. 1. Fall, 1976.

Waring, Gerald A. *Geology and Water Resources of South Central Oregon*. Washington: Government Printing Office, 1908.

INDEX
(Page numbers of photos in black type.)